This Book is Dedicated to the Memory of Warren Claus

This book is dedicated to Warren Claus. Warren passed on Tuesday May 2, 2017 at 32 years of age.

I believe in truth and justice

I treat everyone with respect

I trust in a higher power

In hopes that everything will not go sour

Through equality

Motivate to create

Laugh, the problems pass

Letting all too just be, to see

Dedication

Humor

Honesty

Creativity

And Compassion.

Grasping everything as a lesson

Free of judgement

For contentment.

The above is a mission statement that Warren wrote during one of the groups he attended at the Canadian Mental Health Association-Middlesex. The words that flow through this mission statement really highlight the type of individual he was. Warren was extremely compassionate and had so much love and wisdom to share. He was free of judgement and was always willing to provide his friends and anyone who crossed his path positive encouragement.

Warren was instrumental to this book project. He was part of the original six individuals who defined the project parameters and he trained to conduct the interviews. Warren conducted a number of the interviews included in this book. What is missing is Warren's own story of lived experience. As a writer he wanted to pen his own story but he became busy with other commitments and then…

Warren was extremely intellectual and was stimulated by meaningful conversation. He was always striving for growth and really took in everything he learned. Warren also had an amazing sense of humor. His smile and charm would light up the room. As well as being a part of the initial group, Warren was part of the last group to work on this project, the group which decided the book name. Warren did not like the working title and suggested This Does Not Define Me: Lived Experiences of Mental illness in its place. After oodles of discussion and after four-rounds of votes it was decided.

Everyone gravitated towards Warren's presence. Despite his struggles, Warren was resilient and continued to face his many challenges. He never gave up hope. Warren's passing was a loss to all that knew the true Warren…, he is greatly missed.

Michelle Philips- Mental Health Worker: Community Wellness Programs London.

This Does Not Define Me: The Lived Experiences of Mental Illness

Introduction

This Does Not Define Me: The Lived Experiences of Mental Illness is a book in the making. Much time has been spent working on this project and herein present the insights.

Actuated by a group of clients of CMHA Middlesex, it is a discerning, diverse anthology. A journey through the mental illness stories of men and women from all walks of life. This is a powerful collection of stories which have been transcribed from a number interviews of clients of CMHA London and surrounding area over the course of four years.

It is earthy and heart- felt, swells of ideas and feelings will overtake the reader. A complex intersection taking shape and a descent into mental illnesses. A snapshot of life and identity. The distinctive voices or narrations for the purpose of inspiring, educating, and illuminating and assisting others to find resolve. It suggests new ways to approach the consciousness of how individuals see themselves. All in all, to make a difference.

This Does Not Define Me, allows incomparable insight into another individual's state of depression, mania, schizophrenia, obsessive compulsive disorder, bipolar, eating disorders, and suicidality. For many a trip through Hell and back. These are people not cases. Survivors not victims. Each individual is different; how they step-up to live purposeful lives and maintain equilibrium on their own terms. On occasion ironic humor is present to personalize each story.

The individuals featured in the book This Does Not Define Me take hold and will not be written off by cruel indifference. These are people speaking out for the first time in their own words. Battling against rampant discrimination and indifference towards understanding and acceptance. Recovery is a relatively new term. This Does Not Define Me lifts the curtain to show each person's step through childhood, diagnosis/ misdiagnosis, treatments (not being pre-packaged and losing sight of the individual), the rough crest of hospitalization, the consequences of self-medication/ addictions. It then sheds light on what part family and friends play through-out the journey to a recovered state. It demonstrates the terrible stigmatization and discrimination experienced by some, and the merciless poverty or homelessness some had to endure. Through it all it is important that each individual does not become isolated or traumatized. Life lessons are learned by the doing, and so they learn to know the warning signs.

Mental illness is a badge of courage. There are indeed high profile persons who have a mental illness. Princess Diana, Rosie O'Donnell, Abraham Lincoln, Virginia Wolfe, Einstein's son, and others. The line between mental illness and so called normality is barely a line at all.

One in five people will have mental illness impact their life in some way. You cannot tell by looking at a person if they are dealing with a

mental illness. Mental illness is not so much a sickness, it is a chemical imbalance of the brain. Substantial compelling stats underlie stories where mental illness prevail. On average 80% are unemployed, reducing them to poverty and putting them in the margins of society. It is a conservative estimate that one quarter of the homeless or displaced persons are mentally ill, as are one-fifth of the prison population. Undaunted their defenders who are living through it come out of the shelter to give full expression to what everyone of us should pay attention to. We are—all of us—constantly in the process of coming into being. We swing, we slide, and we are still. Here in This Does Not Define

Me: The Lived Experiences of Mental Illness we have a collection of incomparable realities saying, "This has happened to me." let what is substantial astonish the world.

By CN

A Few Issues to Please Note

1. Please be aware that these stories of lived experience are written verbatim and can therefore be quite raw in language. To maintain the integrity of the project the language was not sanitized and as a result could be triggering. Take care with yourself as you read through the book.

2. Canadian Mental Health Association Middlesex (CMHA Middlesex) came into existence in 2014. Prior to that WOTCH, CMHA London, and Search Mental Health in Strathroy were three Community Mental Health Provider in this region. As part of the three legacy organizations that amalgamated, all references made by the individuals featured is now CMHA Middlesex.

3. London Psychiatric Hospital (LPH) is now referred to as Parkwood Institute: Mental Health Care Building (PWMH)

4. You might notice as you read through these stories that all titles for individual's mental health concern—such as depression—are not capitalized. This was not in error, it was decided that to do so would continue to emphasis the illness and not the individual.

Determination and Moving Forward: The Story of Aimee Fischer

My journey through mental illness started when I was in middle school. At age thirteen, I realized I was becoming depressed, and beginning to have suicidal thoughts. I didn't tell a solitary soul about the way I was feeling and so I became more anxious. I could not take it any longer and in my last year of high school I finally got help. I asked a guidance counselor to help me and I went to my family doctor that same day. That was when I was diagnosed with major depression.

I really struggled in my last semester of high school. I didn't know how I was to going to survive until graduation. I only needed two more credits to graduate. I worried I could not do it. But I managed to complete those two credits and I graduated. Then my journey into university began. I decided that when I was in university I would not tell anyone about my battle with mental illness.

Mental illness has really impacted my life. Sometimes I felt like it was tattooed on my forehead. All my classmates in high school knew that I was struggling with it. Kids from my school would find out and talk about my illness to their parents and then their parents would phone my mom and want to talk to her about it. This is how my mom found out I was cutting myself.

I been hospitalized five times. First in 2002, then in 2003, again in 2011, then in 2012, and finally in 2013.

When I went to university I was nervous. University life can be challenging for anybody, and it was incredibly so for me since I had a mental illness. I did not know how to care for my mental health. While I was at university I was diagnosed with obsessive compulsive disorder (OCD) I was a real 'checker.' I checked everything and anything. It would take me half an hour to leave my apartment because I would have to check everything. I would get out of the door and think to myself that I had not checked everything. Then I would have to go back into my apartment and I would start my whole routine of checking over again. I have received one on one treatment for OCD for approximately three years. Today I still struggle with this conditions. I don't like to touch things since I feel they are contaminated. However, it is a lot better than it was.

During my last year of university, I was diagnosed with bipolar disorder. In a way, I felt relief, but that started a long, long struggle to find the right medication. I was put on Lithium and the side effects for me were bad.

Since I struggled at university, I decided to switch to a Continuing Education program. It was the right decision I graduated and moved to London. I got a job at a retail store. Then I moved on to a job at a bank. The work environment at the bank was toxic. While I was working there I had to go on short-term disability because I had a huge manic- mixed- episode. When I came back my colleagues and supervisors didn't treat me the same way. So I ended up quitting after ten months. I was depressed and suicidal again. I didn't want to go on with life.

In 2002, I was admitted to Homewood Health Center in Guelph Ontario into the Core Program. On my first day there I cried. It was a whole different experience for me. I had to sign myself in and out on a whiteboard. They wanted to know where I was going and the times for when I would leave and return. At the end of each day they locked the doors on all the floors. Then each night they did hourly checks where they came around with a little flashlight to check in on me.

In a way this routine created a false little world. When it came time to be discharged I didn't want to leave Homewood; yet I didn't want to be there either. It was an awkward situation. The day I was discharged also was the first day of my second year of university. So I left the hospital and was really quite upset. I didn't want to go back to university but I knew I wanted to get on with my life. I was so confused.

I was admitted to Homewood hospital for the second time during the summer of 2003, after my second year at university. I was really suicidal. This time I was placed in the Acute Care Unit. It was ten times worse than the Core Program. Lucky for me it was a short stay. I think it was about a week in duration.

My third stay, in 2011, was on the seventh floor of Victoria Hospital, here in London. That, let me tell you, was one of the hardest, longest, and most painful hospital stays I have had. I went in because my psychiatric medicine was causing me to have Parkinson-like symptoms. The movement neurologist realized that my medication was not right and that I needed to go off it otherwise the tremors I was experiencing might become permanent. I was terrified. No one wants to hear that their medication-induced symptoms could become permanent, and that those symptoms resemble those of a sixty-eight-year-old woman with Parkinson's disease.

So I ended up with a new psychiatrist, who switched my medication and let me go home. Within a couple of days I noticed I was no longer sleeping and had high agitation. I was delusional in my thoughts. I was re-admitted to the hospital and placed on the psychiatric ward. My parents came to see me. I will never forget the look on both their faces. It seemed to question what was going on with me.

I thought I was just going in to have my medication adjusted: I ended up spending over seven weeks there. I became extremely delusional. In my delusion I thought my roommate was trying to kill me; saw bugs flying through the air; soap flowing from the washing machines down the hall; men in hazard suits coming to clean it up; and police officers coming to arrest me. My family had no idea what was happening to me. As my parents said "You didn't go in like that."

I now know what triggered all the delusional thinking. One night, while in the hospital, I went into the bathroom that my roommate and I were sharing, and she was cutting herself. There was blood everywhere. Her night gown was soaked in blood. I went running down to the nurses' station and told the nurse there that the bathroom floor was covered in blood. The nurse tried to reassure me that it was just red candy wrappers on the floor. After that I was totally convinced my roommate was trying to kill me and I refused to sleep in our room.

Every night I made a fuss and wouldn't sleep. A nurse called my mom and asked her for some help and advice. My mom did not know what to do but she asked the nurse to put me on the line. My mom patiently told me to just go to bed and get some sleep. Then mom and dad would come to see me on the following day. She convinced me I needed to listen to the nurses and just go to bed. So I did, but it was tough and I was scared.

That particular night was a difficult night but my parents were so patient, nice, and caring. They lived in St Thomas, and drove to London and back every day so they could spend two or three hours with me. That was really nice of them to do that. I know they really cared.

After seven long, painful, and difficult weeks of not sleeping, not eating, and sometimes having arguments with the nurses. To think that my roommate was trying to kill me, to lie in bed all day because I lacked motivation to get out, and feeling completely dark. After seven long weeks of this struggle my mom convinced the nurses to put me into a private room.

My fourth hospitalization was 2012 at Victoria Hospital. I spent six weeks there and it wasn't quite so bad. I was doing really well on my new medication until I became severely depressed. I had to be put on an antidepressant. Then I was discharged.

My last hospitalization occurred in 2013. I was involuntarily committed for a week at the Regional Mental Health facility. The only daylight I saw during that period of time was a half hour on Canada Day. On that day my support team agreed to let my parents take me out onto the grounds. The only other time I left the ward was for about twenty minutes in total, to get my blood work done. That really wasn't a pleasant experience. I really did not like that hospitalization at all.

For me, mental illness resembled what I saw in my grade twelve English class. Mental illness was portrayed in such a negative way in the literature we read. We read a play that ended with the character shooting himself; and the last word in the play was BANG! We also watched the movie One *Flew Over the Cuckoo's Nest.* After that I was certainly not in a hurry to tell anyone that I had a mental illness. I was deeply disturbed by that movie, so I didn't say anything to anybody. I was so confused that I believed what happen in the movies and the books I read was what really happened. Mental illness has been so negatively portrayed in society that I thought it's better to keep it all inside because if I looked for help it would only get worse.

Now for me mental illness looks like determination. It looks like there is hope at the end of the tunnel. There is no template as to what mental illness looks like. People with mental illness come from all walks of life and anybody could get it, at any time. Some people will have a chronic condition for the rest of their lives and some people will have an acute mental illness and suffer for a short period of time. For me, taking medication is OK. At one point I thought I wouldn't want to take medication. The fact is, medication alone won't cure anyone; there is a whole lot more a person needs to do. So for me, I am moving forward and I have people supporting me along the way.

Staying on the Right, Tight, and Clean: The Story of Alicia Finan

I've been diagnosed with schizoaffective disorder.

When I was much younger, I was hospitalized and diagnosed with bipolar type II. Getting sick at a young age was confusing. I never really knew what it meant to have a mental illness. I would be hyper one day and crying the next. Still

this cycling was normal for me; it was all I had ever known of myself. When I would see this behavior in a movie or on the news, I just didn't get it. I did not see the connection. Sometimes I don't get it today.

Being told you have a mental illness at a young age can be hard to accept. I never thought anything was wrong. Even today there are days when I fight it. However, now I realize that I have to be careful to stay on the right, tight, and clean. Now that I am older I see the need for medication and talk therapy. When I was younger I did not see the need to control my behavior so I just rolled with the punches.

Being diagnosed has impacted all areas of my life. It all started when I was so young. I started cutting when I was 11, and people noticed something was wrong. Life was unbearable, so at 15 I started to abuse weed, ecstasy and meth. I was trying to hide the confusion and waves of feelings I had inside. The drug abuse went on and off until

I was 22 years old. The drinking went right along with the drugs and I still to this day struggle with sobriety; a lot.

My condition did not become serious until a year and half ago when I made a bad choice and ended up getting arrested. That really opened my eyes: I needed help and I needed to stay on my medications every day.

When I was 16 or 17 I was hospitalized for my mental illness. That was a really scary experience for me, being so young and not fully understanding what was going on in my head. I was put on medication to stabilize my moods. I was so anxious in the hospital. That was when I first realized something was wrong. I met some individuals in the hospital and we became good friends. Since then I have been in hospital seven different times.

My hospital stays would sometimes be for two weeks, or for a month or longer. I am still frightened when I have to go to the hospital. At the same time I take a bit of comfort because there are others there who have the same struggles. To see them get better creates a hopeful feeling for me. I go in and get checked out every seven or eight months so it's easier and less hectic on my recovery journey.

With the highs and lows of the bipolar component my moods change dramatically, like light frequencies. The other half of my illness includes hearing things as well as having strange body sensations. I have breaks from reality that confuse my abilities to manage my daily living.

When I was arrested I used the mental health Court Diversion program. The program treats both the legal issues and—if the individual agrees—will treat the mental health issues. I completed my full commitment which took a number of years.

Since the beginning of my mental health issues I have been learning how to cope with my reality. My high moods and my low moods. I've learned a lot about myself and have better coping skills and handle my stressors and triggers better.

I have taken a number of programs and workshops so that I can learn what to do when I get sick, and what my warning signs are. It's taken a long time and I'm still learning to this day. I know I have to be careful with stress and getting enough sleep or my whole week gets thrown off. It takes me a while to recuperate from a bad day.

While I was growing up my mental illness scared people away from me. To this day my thoughts, beliefs and behaviors confuse others, destroying many cherished relationships. My mental illness has alienated my sister to the extent that she doesn't want a relationship with me. My condition worried my mom and dad sick; their house became a war zone as I acted out due to mental health issues. They were angry at how I used to treat them. They walked on egg shells for years around me. It's definitely affected their relationship with me and with each other. I feel remorseful, responsible for how we've lived. It has taken a toll on their nerves and they've gotten tired, weary of spending time with me. People, including myself, get confused and many of my relationships are strained.

It's not so scary now. Most days, I see mental illness as a machine: all aspects of our lives have to line up and function for us to stay healthy. We need to find the right balance. We can't run or hide from it. It will always find us.

I am always learning better strategies to live more at peace with my bipolar - schizoaffective disorder. Taking classes at Canadian Mental Health Association Middlesex (CMHA) has been invaluable. I have learned many skills to use in daily living. The social aspect has been wonderful as well. In addition, medications have been important for my recovery. So too has talking with an assigned social worker. I am still learning about my triggers, and how to calm myself down properly.

I wish to give others hope. Mental illness is a challenging, ongoing process. It's okay to take a couple of steps back as long as you continue to travel forward. Never give up on your goals, whatever the setback, because goals help us to move forward. I want others to know that there is always help out there, even though it is scary to reach out and ask for help. I would like people to realize that many individuals struggle with mental illness and we can always help each other.

I had a positive experience happened when I started coming to CMHA Middlesex in London. I discovered that having a mental illness was more common than I thought. It just can't be something you stuff away and ignore. I'm grateful for so much in my life now. I can breathe easy. I can think straight. I can feel confident. I just keep trying to embrace it all.

Alicia Finan, My Good Friend *

Friend who came into my life for a brief time
But will leave a mark
In my life forever
She saw me through
The good and bad times.

Loved the days when I would walk through the door
The light blinking on the answering machine
"Hi Aimee, just Alicia calling…"
Then on she would go
About her day
Or asking me a question or favour.

Often talk to her now
Just to let her know
That I am thinking about her
And letting her know
I know
She is looking down on me
And that she will always be doing that
And one day I will see her
Again.

*I wrote this poem the night before Alicia's funeral as a way to deal with the sudden loss of my good friend.

By Aimee Fischer

Finding Self-Acceptance:
The Story of Alan
Blenkhorn

During my first encounter with mental illness I was certain that I had done something wrong. That I was this terrible person who would be left in the hospital forever. That was it for me, I was now crazy and could not live in society. This was my thinking at the time. However, in time I knew that was not the case. Once I knew what would happen to me I was able to deal with it.

I was first hospitalized when I was 19 years of age for depression. I was living with my parents at the time. They tried to help and support me. My parents found a doctor who I could talk to. But even though I was talking with a doctor, my depression seemed to escalate. I ended up hospitalized because I tried to suicide. I had sunk into a dark place. My thoughts were deep, disturbing, and sinister. That was when the realism of being mentally ill hit me, when I was first on the psychiatric ward.

During that first hospitalization I felt that the people who I came in contact with were not real, that they were an illusion, a figment of my imagination. I was sure that I was somehow in some kind of scenario where I was going to figure something big out or be some kind of hero. I also wasn't very cooperative with the nurses and the other staff and I caused some chaos and so they had to strap me down on to my bed. My worst nightmare seem to be coming true. Within a few days; I started to feel a bit better, and then all I wanted to do was to leave the hospital. That was when I realized that I wasn't going anywhere for a while. I was formed and would have to stay in the hospital for two weeks. You know it's odd, they made me sign those papers when I first came in to the hospital and I didn't know who the hell I was at the time: I thought I was Jesus.

So I continued to follow the hospital procedures and take the medications that were assigned to me. I found myself no longer looking for help; I was just looking to get the hell out of there. I was saying and doing whatever they wanted me to. To me it felt like the medicines and the treatments just made me feel even more miserable.' So now, I was not only fighting with my mental illness, I was also fighting with the pills and the many side effects they caused. Fighting with the nurses because being confined in a hospital for so long is just terrible. I felt like I had done something wrong; I must have, to be in the hospital. Like in some way unknown to me I was a bad person. That I would be left in there forever.

I spent a lot of my time while in the hospital trying to figure out what I could have done to make me feel so bad. Like my mental illness was a direct result of my own bad behaviour. I could come up with a few things such as when I was young I wasn't the best kid or whatever: but I couldn't think of anything I did that was so bad; which would lead to me feeling so awful, and being in that situation.

My big thing was realizing what had happened. What did I do? I can only remember flashes. It was like I was in a dream going through everything that happened. I just didn't believe it was real until they were telling me. They gave me antipsychotics for the first time. They told me along with it that this other pill would help me relax. But the pills didn't help me relax. They simply put me in a cage, a human cage. In my mind I would have to tell my hand to lift-up or to grab-the- fork. I was that out of it. These side effects just made me feel even more mentally ill.

For that first hospitalization I had to stay the two weeks. When they let me out I stopped taking the medicine prescribed to me because it made me feel so horrible. Then I relapsed and I ended up in jail. I was in jail for four months. My mental health was not stable while I was jail. They had to put me in solitary confinement and they put me on what's called a suicide watch. I was forced to wear this blanket, it was like a big thick blanket, and it sort of brushed up against your skin. It was just the most uncomfortable thing. I was humiliated.

In jail there were a few guards who didn't have the patience for me. They were mean to me. So I just played it tough and didn't care. The guards would beat me up for saying something smart or trying to be cool. It was all a part of it. I was the 'bad boy.' I was really angry. Soon it became a vicious cycle, the more the guards paid attention to me, the more attention seeking behaviour I exhibited. I became a big pain in the ass. Again, while in jail I felt like I did something wrong. Well I know I did do something wrong or I would not have been in jail. But it was deeper than that. I felt like I did something terribly wrong. So in order to compensate I would act like a real bad ass.

These two events were my first experiences with mental illness. I can say it never got easier. It never changed the way the hospital worked, never changed the way the jails were run. I had to cope and deal with it; on my own, the best I knew how. So, I'd have to say that my first experiences with mental illness were bad, real bad.

After I got out of jail I didn't really have a place to stay. My parents didn't trust me to come back and live with them due to my actions while I was ill. So I found myself living out of the city's Men's Mission. I did would not take the medicine prescribed for me regularly. But I wanted to stay out of jail and the hospital, so I tried the best I could to act like I was stable. Yet I still knew that my behavior was off and I had a feeling that in some way I was responsible for some of the outcomes I faced.

In hind sight I know that I was once again losing my mental stability. But this time around I feel it was my own doing. I wasn't making the effort to get my own place. I wasn't trying to look after myself. I just didn't care. I isolated and I felt like I was a horrible person. That everyone hated me. So why would I bother? Mania and psychosis were setting in again and odd behaviours were becoming harder to hide. It was almost like the psychosis occured because of me, but I am not a part of it. I am the observer. Like there was a viewer inside my head giving commentary and saying 'I'm fine, I don't know what you're talking about, I'm just being funny or I'm just doing this, I'm just doing that.' It was almost like I was on a ride and the ride is me.

I remember wandering the streets confused about where I was. Was I in my hometown or was I in London. I was just lost. Lost in my head. I was lost in the streets. I was picked up by the cops again. I am not really sure what I was doing, but the cops thought I was drunk. Back in a cop car again. But this time the cops realized I was mentally ill and so they took me to the hospital and not to the jail.

I was once again formed, this time for 72 hours. Because I'd been there before I knew the routine. I knew what was going on. I even knew the nurses, the doctors, and the staff. They all knew my behaviors and so the adjustment was eased for everyone. Still, it was starting to seem to me that the hospital became a place to go when my friends and family couldn't handle me anymore. 'Put him in the hospital he obviously needs more help than we can give him.' Then after a few days and a visit with one of the hospital social workers they put me back into the real world and I was supposed to stay out of trouble. It all felt like a big game we all were playing.

At the time I guess I was prejudice when I thought of mental illness. Mental illness looked like what I saw on TV. Those who had a mental illness were serial killers and rapists. You know all the really terrible things that a person can do was all the result of mental illness. Then it is me who has a mental illness and I am in the hospital.

I remember there was a smoke room and everyone would meet there. They would just gab away about what happened to them and we all smoked our cigarettes. If I sat there and just listened they all were talking about the same things. How they ended up in the hospital. I met other mental health patients who were accountants, lawyers, secretaries, and in all other walks of life. Just people, people who were dealing with the same things as me. Who had the same experiences and feelings as me. People who had done nothing bad enough to cause their mental illness.

I had a tough time with the self-acceptance part. I was hospitalized a lot because of my stubbornness and pride. In time it just sunk in that it would be easier if I accepted my illness. And then I educated myself on my illness. Then I could be ahead of the game. It did work for a while. I had a stretch of eight years were I was working and I wasn't on medication or anything and I was fine. I remember coming back to Ontario from Vancouver and it all was happening again. I was becoming unstable. My parents mentioned it and I didn't want to accept it or deal with it. So once again I denied it.

Another hospitalization occurred and this one was nothing like the others. I was admitted to the London Psychiatric Hospital (LPH) and I'd have to stay there for three months. It didn't feel like a hospital, it felt like a place they put 'us-people.' I was sure they would not feed us. The hospital didn't allow me to go outside for walks. And this time the wards were locked down. In time I began to follow the rules laid out for me. I began to do what I was supposed to do. This made my stay a little easier.

It felt like I was doing things on purpose but then sometimes I didn't feel like I was myself. I felt like I was alone, I was being tortured. Again, I felt like something was wrong, I was doing something wrong or I'm like this because of the way I acted or something like that. What did I do to make me so mad? What made me so depressed? I didn't know at all why all this was going on. I was losing everyone who cared for me. No one could trust me. I became an outsider. So negative.

My family also felt the impact of my mental illness. They would try to tell me I was not well and I would push them away. In my mind I was smarter than they were. That I had my mental health issues under control. Later, as I started to feel better I realized my losses. I lost my friends, my girlfriend, and my parents. While sick my behaviours had frightened them and they no longer wanted contact with me. And there it is again. A reason to believe I did something terribly wrong and that I must be a horrible person.

I think I have been hovering for a while on my recovery. Maybe the last stage of my recovery. I think I am dragging it out because I am afraid to take the next step. To do so would mean more responsibility. I'm just at the point where I still get depressed and I still have problems associating with the general public because of a number of phobias. Also, today I have issues with being outdoors. It's like every time I've gotten in to trouble I was outdoors and at home I'm just fine—so that's where I am with my recovery—I'm at home.

I find that I talk about my mental health more too. Before I wouldn't want to talk about it at all. I guess I thought if I did people would realize I'm crazy and I still bought into that old stigma. Now, I joke about it and try to make it as real as possible. Thinking about my hospitalizations and stuff like that makes me realize that I was never in control. Now I compare mental illness to diabetes. You have it forever and you learn how to manage it.

I've been dealing with mental health issues for a long time. I denied it for a long time because of stigma. If I had a mental illness it was because I was a horrible person who did something wrong. Once I saw that anyone could have a mental illness I could accept my own. Once I found self-acceptance I could stop fighting the inevitable. I did not need to go through all that and neither does anyone else. If they can just find self-acceptance then they could get support sooner. Just because someone has a mental illness does not mean they are a horrible person. We are all human.

Gifts and Huge Blessings: The Story of Andrew Szemeredy

My first significant brush with mental illness came at age 14, when one day I day-dreamed how nice it would be to be mentally ill. Back then, I had no clue how exactly awful it is to be sick; at the time I idealized mental illness as a sickly heroic condition.

My second encounter with mental illness came at age 19, when one night I dreamt I was mentally ill. In this dream I behaved more like a stroke victim, being speechless and bed-bound. In my dream, people I knew came to visit, and looked at me with pity in their eyes.

The third brush with mental illness started with a violent attempt to kill myself. I had been suffering from an ever-deepening depression since the age of 13. When I was 20 years old, I slashed my veins. I was actively and horribly suffering.

At age 14 I did not want to live any longer. I decided then that non-existence is preferable to existence.

One of the many reasons I rejected the call of Christians to join their faith was their promise of an everlasting live. I wanted my life to end. Period. Full stop. End of paragraph. No everlasting life for me, thank you very much.

Eventually I began to get better. My illness had taken away my social skills. I have regained them ever-so-slowly but, to date, incompletely.

If you ever ask a close relative or family member of a mentally ill person how the person is doing, typically they will say "Oh, Peggy is doing much better, thank you very much. She is starting school this fall, hoping to become a registered manicurist," or something to that effect. We, the mentally ill, always get better and feel better year-after-year, and yet at 40 we feel just as shitty and desolate and incapable and insane as at 20 and at 60, if we even reach that age.

What helps me, essentially, are the gifts and huge blessings from society: I am on welfare, so I don't have to work and can avoid starvation; I take medication, which is very helpful; and I am able to move about in Southwestern Ontario. If I have made myself a completely hated person in one community, then I can always move to a different community.

Being mentally ill is not a bed of roses. It is a debilitating disaster that affects the person suffering from it and his entire family. It is not easy to be a mental patient, and it is not easy to be around a mental patient. The psychiatric profession focuses too much on helping the patient feel better. The field painfully lacks a system where by members of the family can be educated about mental illness. Educating those affected by the presence of a mentally ill person would have a spiral effect for both the patients and their social environment.

I Have Something to Pass On; Experience, Strength, and Hope: The Story of April Reading

My name is April, and one of the facets of my life is that I have been diagnosed with bi-polar. I have so many parts of me that make me who I am, so it is only one part of me. My background is Native, English, and Irish. First I'll tell you about some struggles I have had, then I'll end with the positive experiences and my strengths.

I have had many admissions to hospitals over the years. I've been in some group homes and homes for special care. The homes were located in London, Port Bruce, and Exeter. Those were not easy years. Also, I was misdiagnosed for years. The doctor tried so many medications on me, even an injection in my hip for seven years.

It was such a difficult time for me, as the doctor was trying to get the right combination of medications. I would go off my medication, thinking it was not working, and sometimes I would go off the medication thinking I was okay. Looking back, I thought I did not need to take medication anymore. Today I realize I was okay because I was on medication.

I have experienced clinical depression and very high manias, psychosis and other symptoms that come with mental illness, like paranoia. When I was younger, I used to drink way too much coffee. Too much coffee enhanced the manias. I would then go without very much sleep for about two weeks straight. I could not sit still. I was hyper; believe me, I was all over the place in conversations with others. A friend of our family told me I had been talking to myself in an office while I waited for an appointment.

Those early teenage years were really hard on my family as well. They were there when I was at my worst, when I didn't make any sense at all. My thoughts, feelings, and behaviours were negative and scary at times.

Another important facet of my life is that I am an alcoholic and have experienced street drugs. That added to my distorted mental state as well. I used alcohol, especially, to manage. Drugs had a negative effect on me. I drank alcoholically for 20 years for many reasons. One was to escape from life, and another was I thought I could control my moods with booze. Medication and drinking don't mix. I would stop the medication so my tolerance for alcohol would increase.

Looking back I was a mess: emotionally, mentally, and spiritually. I was broken and hurting. I also experienced a lot of loss in my life. My mom passed away when I was 13. Many years later, I lost two brothers in an eight-month period. They were 35 and 32 years old. One was my twin brother, who died through suicide. My dad and step mom are gone now too. I didn't have any coping skills or daily living skills either.

So now I'm going to tell you about some of my strengths and positives. There are many. One is recovery from alcohol with a program that works for me. I sobered up on July 24, 1996 so this month I'll be sober 20 years. I have an amazing support system in place.

I have so many friends in recovery, which is amazing to me. I also have Canadian Mental Health Association (CMHA) programs where I feel empowered, and my comfort level is so good. I practice self-care as well. I have the love and support of my family, which is huge for me because I care so much for them. I like being a family person too. I have respect for myself and others. I really do like most people. I am quite a happy person (I have my times; they are getting shorter).

My relationships are pretty healthy these days. I haven't been in the hospital for over 11 years: a big accomplishment for me. I do cognitive therapy and write in a journal. I have a mental health team that helps. Through that team, I have a nurse I talk to once a week. I am making a lot of progress with the relationships I have with others and myself too. I am a willing participant to better my life and it helps me to have an open mind to people and their suggestions. The goal is always to get healthier.

I am responsible in all aspects of my life. My medication has been working for over 15 years: finally the right combination. I have been in the same apartment for over 18 years. I pay my rent on time and I pay my bills on time. I keep up with cooking, cleaning, laundry, and all household chores. I can also be there for people when I say I will. I can help others with my empathy and compassion.

Being a healthy sibling makes me happy. I love myself so that's why I can love others. I have made happy memories with people, especially with my family. It is really nice to be there for them. I love the fact that I am a strong person most of the time. I am a loyal, trustworthy friend: that I learned and earned.

I believe it's a sign of strength to ask for help. When I ask I usually get what I need. I love life though sometimes it's not easy. When I have hard times I tap into my inner strengths. I endorse laughter and tears. Both are so healing. I have made progress in all areas of my life. It did take a lot of hard work. Some of the benefits are that I like who I am, and I am comfortable in my own skin.

Someone who worked with me once said to me "the best is yet to come for you." I hope so. If I compare myself to others I know I will not be happy. I measure my own progress. I am extremely happy. What a wonderful journey, with its ups and downs and all arounds. I will always work on myself to get healthier and healthier. That will not stop. I am so grateful to the mentors in my life. Thank God for life: the beauty in nature, animals, and finding soul mates and cherished people that cross our paths. Some people are in my life for a long time and others a shorter time. I like to embrace it this. I like to feel comforted with my pets; they do a good job. My life as it is now is a remarkable adventure.

Connection on a Deep Level: The Story of Beth

I was born in Nova Scotia and was shifted from hospital to hospital through many provinces. My mother and younger sister moved from Toronto to London. At the time I was in Whitby Psychiatric Hospital and they transferred me to London Psychiatric Hospital to be nearer to my family. I was fairly young at the time, about 25, so it was a very enlightening thing for them to do.

My mother bought this little house for me at one point, so I would always have a home to go to. I was very fortunate, and I lived in that little house for 26 years. I know and appreciate how lucky I am. I have got a great family. Medications are another thing entirely. You see, when I was discharged from the hospital I was livid, so angry at the treatment I'd received over the years. It started when I was just 16 and was drugged with chlorpromazine.

I had been diagnosed with schizophrenia. I was subjected to numerous shock treatments. I literally begged the orderly "I'll do anything, anything you want". It was a living nightmare. To top things off, when I was 22, I had a prefrontal lobotomy. The doctor had told my mother it would be my only chance. He said if I did not have it I would be lost forever, somewhere on a back ward, drooling, completely lost. Of course my mother, at the time, did not know any better, for that matter neither did I. I just signed for it and said "I don't care, do whatever you want to me."

After the operation I asked when I would be allowed to leave the hospital. Evidently it takes two or three years before it has the desired effects. I told him "You gave me the impression that after I'd had the operation I could get out." The doctor answered "I never gave you that impression." I told him he was a liar. I grabbed something from his desk and threw it at him. I got locked up in seclusion for that. But it felt great at the time.

There was all manner of lying going on in the hospitals. And the medication caused weight gain, as did all the carbohydrates and sugar in the food. It happened like you wouldn't believe. I know this from firsthand experience.

I was first introduced to Canadian Mental Health Association Middlesex (CMHA) when I was still in hospital. I was told CMHA delivered a series of programs with the focus on groups. When I was released from the hospital I was on a great deal of medication, old style medication that made me feel like a zombie. I imagine the criteria for hiring hospital staff was different than hiring CMHA staff. Life experience mattered a lot more than book learning. That was a very interesting revelation for me because the London Psychiatric Hospital (LPH) dragged me into oblivion. It was maybe not the opinion of the LPH but it was how I felt about it.

According to the doctors at the LPH being over-medicated was good for me because it controlled my symptoms. My symptoms were schizophrenia with delusions and hallucinations. In fact, the symptoms were not controlled by drugs. They never were. My mental illness is extremely resistant to drugs. So it's my belief that I was much easier to handle when I was doped up.

The drugs made me feel tired all the time. It could be pretty terrible. In the early group therapy sessions at CMHA people were on thiazine's, chlorpromazine, and haldol. The doses of medication were so heavy that it took something really gripping to get anyone's attention. At CMHA it was considered very bad form to fall asleep in group. I would hear "Are we boring you Beth?" I would exclaim "It's the drugs. That's what those medications did."

Every week we had a day at CMHA when the doctor would review our medication. The doctor could change meds if he thought it was necessary, but he made sure everyone was taking their meds. I wasn't fond of the doctor. He was certainly a great idea man, but as a personal General Practitioner he sucked big time. So I saw a different doctor. I was the exception.

So when I first started, it was more than just an alternative to hospital, for me it became my haven. The staff who worked with me at CMHA made me feel safe. They were interested in me; they wanted to know how I felt. They wanted to know about my thoughts and dreams. It was all important. I was made to feel cared about as an individual.

In the programs we were taught life skills. Not in an antiseptic lab or classroom, but by doing. In one group we would go shopping for the next week's groceries. In another we would prepare a meal. And yet another group would do the clean-up. I tried to avoid all that though.

The programs started with about 25 people in the morning meeting, and then separated into smaller groups. I can remember it all like it was yesterday. There was one group where we were asked to write about ourselves. We were given magazines. I cut out a picture of a Ferrari. I pasted it on a piece of Bristol board and wrote out "the new model of Beth is sleek and sporty with verve and excitement available nowhere else." This went over well with everyone and I was smug for about a week.

Back then I was involved in the old day programs held at the CMHA Ridout Street site. I was involved with highly structured programs for full days. It was actually various group with group activities and we were encouraged to participate in all aspects of the programs. There were also evening programs run by senior staff at the old Goodwill at Dundas and Adelaide. They were more social. People would show up, and we would play games and sometimes work in the kitchen. There was also creative artistic stuff. Honestly it was just like family. I can't get across how nice it was. It just worked. It clicked. It was just different. I felt connected on a very deep level. It never stopped working until the funding stopped.

Recreation and activity programs ran in tandem with therapy groups. I enjoyed the smaller group set-ups. It was a whole new way of living life. They made me feel safe. It really was a complete haven for me- an anti-asylum. I considered it mine. There was zero tolerance for any violence. We were friendly comrades. We all were.

We did self-evaluations on a regular basis in front of the whole group. As in, 'this is what I am doing, this is what I have achieved, and this what I am going to achieve.' I can remember playing volley ball. No matter how inept a person was, we played with encouragement and laughter. We had real fun. Everyone was expected to have fun, so we did. There was so much humor and laughter. Not the indulgent condescending type of laughter normally delivered for mentally-ill patients, but the real thing. Of course, there was the expectation that all of us would grow as people.

Sometimes I would feel pissed off at the gradualness of change. Then I would become bored with a tired feeling, believing that there was no visible alternative. At CMHA, I was not judged. I was just a true people person. At the 10th anniversary I saw doctors and staff from the hospital. I was not impressed and one of the CMHA workers told me they were guests here for their own edification. It was hard for me but I was nice, darn it. The point was that they were trying to create a bridge between old style and cutting-edge mental health care. There were important politicians there and such. They were attempting to change the future of individuals like me.

I have committed myself to the programs at CMHA Middlesex for 35 years. They've taught me about issues that are relevant: goal setting and engaging in the community; going for walks and excursions to the museum; things that I felt like doing. I am on the big waiting list to do it all over again. As I grow so does the programs I am in. They even had an Ethics in Mental Health Committee comprised of both staff and clients. That's revolutionary. Recovery is not something that just happens. It is a lifelong journey and I will be on that journey until I die. The programs have helped me on that journey.

Beth passed away suddenly on November 1, 2013. Beth lived independently and, while alone in her home, fell, bumping her head and succumbing to her injuries. Beth was a client of CMHA since 1986. She was loved and well respected by all that knew her. She was a survivor and a fighter. Beth had such a way with words, and loved to write. She was always supportive and encouraging to her peers. She could be extremely stubborn or passionate as some might say. She was one feisty woman with a great sense of humour. I loved to see Beth in action when she played on our Baseball Team, and I could listen to her stories about her cats and her trips to San Francisco all day long. Beth was so proud of herself when she was finally able to quit smoking.

I will leave you with a famous quote of Beth's. Whenever you asked her about her well-being, this was her reply: "As good as to be expected under the circumstances in which I currently toil." Beth, rest in peace. You are dearly missed here on earth. Crystal McKellar, Mental Health Worker, CMHA

Welcome the Morning:
The story of CN

It is a warm
summer evening and the
windows are all open, but
still my quixotic meds for
sleep are keeping me
hostage. But no, not again.
When did it last happen:
seven years or seven
months?

In the empty apartment
below me there are three people at it. Sticking up little metal rods
through their ceiling, through the carpet again, up through the box
spring and my eight inch mattress. Impossible poking. And I'm
drenched in sweat.

Now they are entering the utility room where I share a wall with
them. I ball up my fists and hold the pillow to my ears. I can hear
their muffled obscenities and jump into a fetal position in the living
room.

Abracadabra! A model T-Ford chugs up. It is 1924 and the
charmingly tipsy group—women in flappers and men in racing
stripes—clink glasses and come inside. Laughing happily: zoom, I
am back in my apartment.

That woman has a big ring of keys and is trying to get in to do me
damage. A sort of shock settles in me. I am hyperaware. My elderly
neighbor, who speaks no English, comes out to the landing and says
"Buckingham palace is lovely dear but I don't live there." Then
everything stops and I pass out.

At last I welcome the morning. I get up and put the coffee on. I go
quickly into the vacant apartment below. There a no holes for metal
rods. The combination lock is still on the utility room. I take a coffee
and sit out on the back deck and feel remarkably calm. I remember

everything as I always do. The day is so still I can hear the clouds move. At this point in my life the psychotic breaks might be brutal but they can't kill me and there's comfort in that. Then two shrill birds shriek at one another—not my problem to solve.

Beginning Again:
The Story of David
Heddington

At 18 years of age, I was studying manufacturing and engineering technology. I was getting good grades. I had no shortage of friends, and I was involved in sports. Everything was going right for me. Then I started to get behind so I had to take night courses while working at my summer job; ten hours a day six days a week. Plus I was drinking socially with friends. I put a lot of pressure on myself. Then, one Sunday as I was driving, the radio seemed to be talking to me, singing I could and should be a rock star.

It seemed so clear to me. I stopped sleeping, and started making grand plans. I quit work and with my last pay I bought a set of drums. I was all over the place and my parents caught up with me and took me to the hospital. I thought there was nothing wrong. The new me was full of life. I had purpose and kind of forgot about school. I just left the hospital, but the police found me and brought me back.

I was transferred to the London Psychiatric Hospital (LPH; now referred to as Parkwood Mental Health Care). They took all my clothes and belongings away and I was put in a seclusion room. I felt fine and not sick at all, and found the assigned doctor very mean.

After a number of interviews I was diagnosed with Bipolar Disorder. That is when I realized I had a mental illness.

Lithium proved to be the medication that got me released from the hospital. I couldn't go back to school for the second term. I went into a depression. I felt that my mental illness ruined my chances at a career. I fought against it with inner strength.

I was 18 years old and I told myself I could find another job. But everything came down on me again. Different thoughts, different things. The result was that from ages 18 through 21 I spent a significant amount of time in the LPH. I didn't really mind. I could just be sick, get well and go ahead and do things. It became a kind of lifestyle.

Then the very best thing happened to me: I met and married Debbie my wife. She is an amazing and stabilizing force for me. She has seen me through my 15 or so hospital admissions.

I came to the realization that I had to change things: the way I acted, my morals, everything. I realized I really needed to take care of myself. I realized this not too long ago.

At 55 years of age, I felt that way again. Four years ago, I suffered a debilitating manic episode. It hit me so hard that I forgot how to think straight. It was like losing a little chunk of my life right there.

I am now retired. I have new things to explore in my life, new skills, new hobbies. It seems like I am always beginning again but that's okay. I have changed. I am more relaxed. I have good medications. I have a good team at the hospital who support me when I need them.

I do remember though that the LPH used to treat patients quite differently than they do today. Back then they had programs in woodworking, arts and crafts, and bingo; there were dances and there was a gym, things to help your mind and body. Today, it seems all patients do is sit, eat, and drink. My hospitalizations did get my mind back. It wasn't just about being sad and walking around a bit outside. It was more.

Today I suspect it is budget cuts. But I came a long way from a One Flew Over the Cuckoo's Nest scenario (The title of the fictional book by Ken Kesey about life lived on a mental ward during the 1970s). I am not wandering the streets or being locked up or hidden away somewhere. I used to think that mental illness was something to be ashamed of. I have come a long way.

Today I see a primary doctor and a social worker. I can talk to either about the problems I am experiencing. They surround me and understand me. They never just brush me off. I have good medications and my doctor takes time to fully explain them to me. If they need any adjusting or adding, I am aware why the doctor is making these changes.

I have been emotional at times, and they have seen me in crisis situations from the sickness. I realize I have to take baby steps with my emotions. With Bipolar Disorder I can get manic, and we treat that. I can get depressed, and we treat that. It is very hard to sustain the in-between, to keep things level. I am learning to problem solve.

I've had episodes of totally falling apart, collapsing and losing consciousness. I've been unable to tie my shoe laces. I've been unable to think straight. Being in the hospital I have lost stretches of time. It is scary.

I don't accept being limited in what I can do. I am retired so I have new opportunities. Once upon a time, all I wanted to do was support my family. I was determined I could function like a normal person. Whenever I applied for a job I never put down that I had a mental illness or had spent time in hospitals. I would work fine for a while but would go in the hospital for what I called a tune-up. I'd get an adjustment or new medication. Then going back to work? Well, even my friends were not my friends anymore. To say the least it was hurtful and damaging.

I ended up leaving jobs because they did not want me back. I felt like an outcast. I was a hard worker and dealt with people so I became self- employed with Q Cabinet Company. But the illness kept coming down on me, no matter what. Just when I seemed to move forward I would move backwards. I have been hard on myself because it is ingrained in me that a man has to work. Every job I did, I worked my hardest. I am secure in that. Right now I am getting back into writing. I've written children's stories and poetry. I also enjoy art and creativity. I am a good house husband. My wife Debbie works.

I am a vegan. I have great recipes and do all kinds of casseroles, stews and soups. Cooking is very relaxing and centering. I like coming to Canadian Mental Health Association (CMHA) for the art courses, writing workshops, and keeping my eye on the front board of the Queens Ave Site for anything that looks interesting.

I liked the anti-anxiety course I took there. I also like baseball. I talk to other individuals with mental illness, which is another good coping skill. It helps both parties. When I took the Life Management Course, it was a good antidote to the hospital. I was with good people in a good place. It was good for my mental health to follow a daily schedule.

My team helps me to try to keep my moods level. But it is a struggle for all concerned. I am over 50 years old and it's not stigma I am dealing with, just frustration. Since I was young I have always had the ability to recover. I've had strength that way. I also recover because I am married. Debbie is my touchstone, my number one fan. I love her and want to take care of her as much as she takes care of me. Despite everything my relationship with my wife keeps getting better.

After all this time, I have to be flexible with my illness; I have to adapt to different situations. That will help my mind and protect myself because I am not the same young person that I was. I used to be so angry about my situation. But with CMHA I have sorted myself out and am a lot more peaceful now.

We Can Cope: The Story of Duncan Woolford

My family sat down one day when I wasn't there, when I was in the hospital, and said "We think he's got a mental illness or something." I was diagnosed with depression and anxiety. When I heard the diagnosis I wanted to cut my wrist.

I was born in 1962 and have been endured a lot of emotional pain. People have called me all sorts of real bad names, like stupid, and fucking retard, and stuff like that. One day I got in a fight and my mom got a phone call from the school. I said to one of the teachers, "I have had enough of this and if you don't like it fuck you."

One day a lady came from the Ministry of Ontario, and told my mom "Put your son in an institution." My mom told her to get out of the house. There was no way she was going to but in some institution. I am doing better today. I'm on medication, and I feel so much better. Since I've been diagnosed I like to say people with mental illness can cope with it, and I'm sticking up for everybody who is dealing with mental health issues. We have to stand up for our rights, instead of being put down.

I didn't like hospitalization. Even when I went to the bathroom they opened up the door to see what was going on and stuff like that. One of the doctors said to me "You are lucky you got help." I have been depressed for the last three and a half years. When my mom wasn't home I just wanted to get a knife and cut my wrists. I never did.

I grew up with a learning disability and everybody put me down. Even today my mom said to me, "You won't be able to do CPR." But I did and I passed.

Since I was diagnosed with mental illness, all my friends say "See you later." I have been put down so many stinking times. I am thoroughly pissed off about it. It's frustrating, I get so angry. I was so upset that I attacked my own father and beat him up. I didn't know what I was doing. After my dad calmed down and I calmed down, I said "I'm sorry dad." It's hard when a family member like me has mental illness. Even my brother said it's alright Dunc, everybody has a disease.

I have a friend who lives on my street with the same illness as me, depression and anxiety attacks. She told me "If you have any problems with your illness, pop on over and we can sit and talk about it." That's good. I have friends across the street from me, plus my mother. My brother asked me how I cope with mental illness. I said "There's a lot of good medication out there for people with mental illness."

My recovery is going slowly because I'm in rehab. I come to CMHA on Fridays. I stay here for lunch and we do stuff in the afternoon. I also go to relaxation class, and it's great.

My positive experience with my recovery is being happy. I take my meds every morning. After I took my meds this morning I sat there and had a couple cups of coffee and a couple cigarettes, and my day was good. I went down and cleaned up a bit in my room. I love coping with the illness I have. Everybody has problems. Albert Einstein had a mental illness. Way back in the civil war of the United States, President Lincoln also had mental health issues. People with mental illness need to get help. Call the mental health crisis line or the distress centre or 911.

A Long and Difficult Road: The Story of Ilse Grills

Well my journey started when I was about seven years of age. It's kind of been an ongoing thing for me, starting with depression and difficulties when I was a child. It just got worse as life went on for me. I experienced various, I guess you would say incidents throughout my life. So it's been a long and difficult road, I'm finally getting the assistance that I need. I am hoping I can heal from most of it. I think it's going to take a long time though. I am still working on it.

I've had stuff happen since I was three years old. I was molested and raped when I was three. I still have nightmares and dreams from that, I mean that's something that is probably going to fade but never go away completely. Something traumatic like that you just never lose. My father occasionally beat me and my mom was mentally abusive. It was a lot for anyone to deal with, and I was not the exception.

I have had my three kids taken from me by Children's Aid, literally ripped out of my arms and then adopted out from under me. They have classified me; I am told, as an unfit mother. This means I'm not allowed to have children under 16 years of age around me unless I have somebody supervising. I mean it's literally been an ongoing thing that just piles up.

Once, after I lost my youngest son, I tried something very, very, very stupid. I took half a bottle of my antidepressants and a giant spoon of peanut butter, which I am allergic to. I ended up in the hospital from this suicide attempt, but I didn't stay there very long. I'm one of those types of people that hit rock bottom, crash, and afterwards start bouncing off the walls. It's like my attention deficit hyperactivity disorder (ADHA) has been held back. I seem to be happy-go-lucky, bubbly person. And so for a suicide attempt I spent just over one week in hospital because they did not understand I was hiding my sadness. They pretty much said; you seem to be fine now, here's your medication, off you go. We will readjust your dose and put you on something to help out and you can go home now. Not much help. I felt as bad as ever.

Since I was 20 I've tried to find help for my mental health issues. I'm now 34. I believe I have fallen through pretty much every crack you can think of. If it wasn't for my ex-husband I wouldn't be getting the assistance I am now. I got a diagnosis of chronic mild depression. Originally, this diagnosis wasn't bad enough to get services. From what I've been told. Now, they've pretty much said I have an undefined mood disorder. It's like, oh wow that's all. It's all good, but I have no idea what it means.

Along with the diagnosis of an undefined mood disorder, the doctors suspect I also deal with post traumatic stress disorder (PTSD) because of the stuff I've been through. But right now it is still just a theory. I'm working on trying to get an assessment done through my psychiatrist essentially to find out what the hell it is so that I can really start the healing process. When I was younger I just thought I had a major case of the sads and I'd be fine. Everybody said "Oh you'll get over it." So that's what I thought as well. So now that I see it from an adult perspective. It definitely blows away a lot of the stigmas.

Growing up I thought somebody who had schizophrenia was automatically crazy and should be locked away. I mean there are stigmas like that all over the place. Well, today I know people who are dealing with this illness and as long as they takes their medication they are perfectly stable. I know someone who has bipolar disorder, the rapid cycling kind. Her mood switches fast but she is not so different. For me I've kind of lost all those stigmas. I know anybody can get a mental illness. An ordinary person can get this and it can just hit unexpectedly. A person has to deal with it and try to heal from it.

My mom still denies I have any kind of mental illness. As far as she is concerned I'm full of it and all I need to do is get over myself. It's really hard to say how it's impacted others in my life because of the fact that everybody else in my life has already been impacted one way or another. My brother is developmentally delayed so he doesn't quite get it but he's supportive. My mom thinks that I need to get over myself. My sister gets it as well. Most of my family and friends get it or at least what's left of the friends and family that I have.

I've recently gotten in contact with a friend who lives in St. Catherine's. I haven't seen him in quite a few years. He's not too sure what to make of me having a mental illness. He's still a little bit weary of it. I can understand why but it doesn't seem to be having as much of an impact as I thought it would. So for me, the people that are closest to me already have had dealings with it because they've had to deal with it themselves or they've been around it for most of their lives.

But I don't think I've fully accepted my mental illness. I mean I know I need help, I know I need assistance and I know I need to deal with it. That's something I've been trying to do for many, many years with little to no success. But for me, it's kind of always been there so there's really been nothing to accept. You know, for me it's just something that is an ongoing thing. When it gets worse I'll hide in a closet and starve myself. That is a sign that it is really bad. But I'm always at a low grade depression anyways. So for me that's just something normal, there's nothing really to accept. It is the way it's always been.

Well, as far as discrimination from other people, it's really hard for them to tell. I mask my illness well. People describe me as having a bubbly personality, but inside I feel the total opposite. I don't want other people to think of me differently. If I didn't have that type of mask and that type of bubbly personality I don't think I would be able to get through it.

Falling through the cracks makes me feel discriminated against. I was somehow not bad enough to need services. "Yah you're not bad enough, so you're on your own. Screw you." That's exactly what it felt like for me. I felt the discrimination came from the way mental illness was handled for some people that weren't considered "bad" enough to receive services. I found that discrimination was in the mental health field itself, not from other people.

Today the Mental Health Care System is a lot better. I was introduced to CMHA by a friend of mine. He recognized that I was not doing well.

That's when the staff at CMHA helped me through the process. I did a self-referral. I knew if I had to go through my family doctor or a psychiatrist that I would not be helped. They would not understand. They would just look at me and think I was fine and decide that I don't need services. So the self-referral thing was a big thing for me. It makes me feel like I'm being heard, acknowledged, not like I'm just somebody that's falling through stupid cracks because people don't listen. So today I feel that I'm being heard, that I'm being listened to, and that this support will eventually help me heal. It's a wonderful thing, I love the idea that I got the self-referral now.

I'm still trying to figure out most of what is going on. I'm dealing with most of the symptoms day to day pretty much. Medication does help but there are days when it's difficult to get out of bed and I still force myself to do it anyways. But I figure things will get better as time goes on.

Mostly I want to let people know that even if they seem to think that finding help is difficult, there is always some avenue. There are services, even if you have to knock on that door yourself. The services are there. You need to find them. There are people out there willing to help you find those services. You just have to ask.

I think that's what a lot of people have difficulty with, is asking. Asking for assistance. My situation as good example. First having difficulty getting services and then finally getting the services I needed through my own efforts. And you don't need to go to your family doctor to get it. You can get it yourself if you need to.

So for me the positive experience is being heard. You know, I'm being heard now, and that's the most positive thing I can really say and literally the first step to my recovery. It's an amazing thing knowing that if I need someone to talk to, my worker is here. She's just a phone call away. You know, it really does make things so much better. Just don't be afraid to ask for help. That's my message: don't be afraid to ask for help.It is there if you need it. You know, seriously, go for it, it's there. If you need to heal it's there. Don't stew in it by yourself; if you need the help get it. It's available for you.

A Change of View: The Story of Jeff K.

I have come to discover that the journey of mental illness recovery doesn't stop once you're feeling stable. It continues. At this point you have to start rebuilding your life as you once knew it while leaving out all the thoughts, emotions and substances that contributed to your own personal downfall.

It's a hard road but once you make the choice to take it you just have to keep going.

There are pitfalls; there are tragedies; there are good times; and there is fun and happiness. There is work; there are responsibilities; and there is stuff to fix, and lots of things that need to get done. I'm two years into my life post-hospitalization and I'm still not caught up. But since trying to get caught up and always feeling like I was behind are the kinds of thoughts that I know have made me unwell in the past. I am choosing to leave them there and just keep going.

The journey's direction and focus are ever changing, with detours and diversions, but I can see now that there is a life and a path that continues on.

Entering the hospital was a terrifying experience. My family told me that I was not well and asked me to go to the hospital. I knew there was something wrong, however I was no longer capable of determining my own reality. I had stopped making any kind of logical sense to those around me and I didn't know what I feared most: I feared everything. Someone could have given me a soft cuddly teddy bear and I would have questioned their motives. So yes, entering the hospital was scary.

Being in the hospital was where I needed to be. I needed rest from the turmoil. Traumatic, negative and inconclusive thoughts had started to control me day-to-day, and had worn me out so much so that I felt there was no point going on. I didn't have a plan for suicide but accidents were high on my wish list.

The hospital was where I made some critical first steps to getting where I am today. I had people available 24/7 to talk to; I don't remember what I said to them and I really didn't trust them at the time, but I accepted early on that I needed help. I was told that the London Health Science Center (LHSC) was the place to do it.

In hindsight, I had deserted myself emotionally, and was starting to question my own identity and place in the world. I thought I was being monitored, I thought that the things people said to me, however unrelated, were somehow connected and it was my determination to connect and question, distort and make all these external stimuli fit into a framework of what I perceived (incorrectly) was happening around me. Then I took action to protect myself from that same framework that had manifested as something that terrified me to my very core. Circular thinking. Downward spiral.

The hospital was great. Meals were important. I ate regularly and gained weight. I got new medications that helped me experience all the stages of sleep. I couldn't relax until a year ago, but the hospital let me rest and that's what I needed. Thank you to the staff there.

My family and everyone I have known for years have been touched by this, some worse than others. Addressing all the hurt, both the perceived hurt that I have felt, and the hurt that I have caused people, is the single hardest thing for me to deal with. I wish in my heart that I could go back and change everything I have ever done that made anyone feel hurt, unloved, scared or uncared for. It still knots my stomach up sometimes when I think about my impulsive actions and angry reactions.

My family lived with me while I was like this. There is no amount of acceptable apology that I could dream up to say how sorry I am to my son and my wife for having to live with me while I was becoming unwell. The major problem is that my becoming unwell happened over decades. I used to focus on making everything right again which is really circular thinking because you can't go back and change history. You can however ensure that it doesn't repeat itself. And that is my apology to everyone who loves me: a pledge to them and myself that I will keep my illness in check and never become the person that I fully remember being and hating.

Mental illness affects your whole life. It's not just the part where you end up in the hospital or try to end your life. I had an idea that I wasn't doing well two years before anyone else did, and regrettably I chose not to act. I pushed it down and kept pushing on, slowly losing control. I started to isolate and alienate; I started to push everyone away, to keep myself and them safe. I believed the world was better off if I distanced myself from it.

I lost my job; I lost my will to work; I lost my means of support. With that came more fear of losing my house, my stuff and everything I had worked so hard to achieve. My employer placed me on short term disability (STD). I couldn't concentrate on my work anymore because my mind was an extremely loud and chaotic place. Losing my job stripped me of purpose and took away any remaining confidence that I had left that I could get through this. Then I was left with nothing to do and no will to do it anyways. 90 days on STD—not better yet—what's the point? I'm fucked. I give up. Hospital. There is so much collateral damage that I am still, to this day, trying to repair it. Not only repairing my own emotional and mental state but my life and role as a father, husband and a fundamentally productive human being. It touches all of it and makes a terrible mess that takes years to put back in order. Piece by piece, day by day.

I assumed that the mentally ill were those on the street, the homeless and the ones yelling at no one in particular. Something was 'not right' with them. As if anything is 'right'?! I always felt sorry for these people but I assumed, incorrectly, that their behaviour was made with logic and reason.

I was too far gone by the time I started having homeless fantasies. Those close to me started to notice that I was muttering to myself and seemed more distant, disassociated and dislocated from reality. What they were seeing was just the tip of what I was experiencing.

My view of mental illness and wellness has changed. Now I understand all too well how individuals get to the point where yelling and muttering to themselves seems a rational thing to do. Live in a cardboard box under a bridge? Sure! There are no people around so you can live with a completely irrational view of what you feel you need to do. You are free. Or at least that is what you are telling yourself—and it all seems good and warm and peaceful until—and this is what most people don't understand about the degradation of mental health—you actually believe that a cardboard box, alone with your thoughts, is your best option. At this point, those thoughts that you so wanted to be alone with slowly erode the fabric of your soul until you don't care what happens anymore. Now, I hate to think anyone should have to live like that.

I have been fortunate to meet people with all kinds of disorders. It is my experience that everyone has the potential to overcome challenges but the special ones that so often get labelled and stigmatized are often the ones that are so close to their own feelings that they will be better people because of it.

Most people I've met are highly artistic: musicians, writers and painters, as am I. I wonder if the lack of importance our society has for these deeply personal things might be doing a disservice to people who identify with anything outside of what society sees as 'normal'. If what we feel in our heart has no value then we have no worth. That is so sad and needs to be changed.

The biggest and hardest part of accepting mental illness is that it actually happened. There is still a part of me that will never let go of the amount of hurt and disappointment I feel about the amount of time and the amount of my life that I have spent feeling terrible.

My life has been touched by mental illness since day one. I question myself constantly asking "Could I have prevented this?" Hindsight forces me to examine my life and to relive all the mistakes and missed opportunities. If I had had the insights I have now, I could have reacted in different ways or simply just made different choices. Then, at least the impact of my actions might have been less.

Acceptance has morphed into knowledge and experience. I now know and understand some of the distorted thoughts caused by terribly low self-worth preceded by many years of living with the tendency to lean toward negative thought. Discrimination and prejudice happen everywhere regardless of anti- this and anti-that legislation. A group of people can easily align against an individual or group. I can't say that I was directly discriminated against and prejudice is too broad a term. From my point of view, the atmosphere of my workplace contributed greatly to my overall mental state. It was an unhelpful and unhealthy environment, full of gender inequality. I have been out of this environment for more than two years. I can honestly say that this abhorrently sexist and racist atmosphere, much akin to a high school locker room, had a significantly negative impact on my overall well-being.

While I can't put my finger on any concrete acts of malice, I do know that I felt an underlying state of fear and panic in this environment on a daily basis. This caused my interaction with people to become tainted and skewed. This atmosphere of passive-aggressive exclusion caused my reactions to external stimuli to become increasingly self-protective. I was very much beginning to feel like the odd-man-out, and I was always questioning and rethinking everything that I was taking in and trying desperately to make sense of it. In the end, I couldn't make sense of anything. To this day I feel that my depression worsened by merely being in this environment for almost twenty years. Looking back I can see and understand the early stages of my descent into psychosis. From the bottom of my soul, I am so much better off and happy that I don't have to go to that workplace again.

I am two and a half years into my life after I hit ground zero. I am still not 'operating' at my previous level. Of late I have begun to accept that 'operating' as I was probably wasn't good for me in the first place. So that leaves me with a paradox of trying to find my way through life again while having to sift through and relearn many of my own fundamental psychological processes. One is completely interdependent on the other. In short, I'm learning how to be me all over again, as the first version self-destructed.

To you, the reader; I hope that after reading this, something I have written has helped you to understand yourself better and to understand that you are not alone. You are a good person and you are worthy of everything your heart desires. You are beautiful in your failures and confident in your achievements. Just keep going and be really, really good to yourself. In my experience, being good to yourself is the one fundamental that gets lost in the shuffle of life.

It's such a freeing feeling to praise yourself for all the millions of things that make you great instead of beating the crap out of yourself for everything you think you did wrong. It's OK. Let it go, be at peace and take time to enjoy the hell out of everything!

This Gift: The Story of
John Hancock

I was not diagnosed with a mental illness until 1999-2000, when I went into the hospital. Since that time it's been an up and down journey. At the moment, I believe the journey helped shape me into the person I am today. I think I'm a better person today than I was 10 or 12 years ago. I used to look in the mirror drunk, and wonder what's wrong with me. Who am I? I didn't realize it at the time, but that was a symptom of my mental illness. When I got diagnosed and got the rudimentary medication, I could look back on it and think okay that's why. I'm better today. The journey has been quite enlightening. It's been a path of knowledge for me.

I think I've had four hospitalizations. The first time I went into the hospital was for the 28-day program. The second time was because of probation; I had a little trouble with the law. So that's been part of my journey too, the court system and the law.

In the past I judged mental illness by what I saw in movies and on television. People were crazy and they weren't part of society. They have the attic up in the old house where they kept crazy grandma; I thought only senior citizens had mental illness, such as dementia. I didn't know that mental illness is a diagnosed disease. I thought it was an action. Now I know it's a chemical imbalance in the brain. It can also have something to do with what happened during childhood; if there was abuse when a child was growing up. The first five years are important. If those first five years are dysfunctional, that could haunt a person in their early teens. That's what happened to me.

I used to play guitar and entertain people. I went back to school to get my grades 11 and 12 so I could get into college. I got a scholarship the first year, and graduated with a 3.68 grade point average.

When I found out about my mental illness, I tried to help other people, and to be more compassionate and empathetic. People with mental illness happen to have this gift of picking up on another person's mental illness. I've been happy to have people with mental illness in my life to help me along with my journey.

Early in my sobriety I was lucky enough to have some after care and some programs to help keep my dignity. That's how I got associated with CMHA, and got into the trauma group which met at Victoria Hospital.

The first hospitalization was when I was in trouble with the law. I had to go get help at the alcohol unit at the St. Thomas Psychiatric Hospital. I was in a 28-day program at the unit. Before that, I had a couple of impaired driving charges. So, I spent a night in jail. When I was in the hospital at the unit for alcoholism I had a nurse who would come around and instead of knocking politely and telling me that snack time was on, she would bang on the door and scream. So that was my first hospitalization. It was court ordered.

The last time I was in the hospital, I was in for three weeks. My post-traumatic stress disorder got triggered by having bed bugs. I said I want to kill myself. As a result my mom got me a condo. The hospital staff helped me with medication, and hooked me up with support programs through CMHA and Can-Voice. So I can see that my last hospitalization, though a negative thing at the time, turned out to be a positive thing at my discharge. I got access to programs that normally I wouldn't be able to have access to, because I needed to be referred. I got a psychiatrist who was instrumental in getting me my Ontario Disability Support Program (ODSP). When I was on Ontario works I didn't have much dignity. With my ODSP, there's much more dignity in everyday life.

As a kid, growing up I always felt there was a stigma around mental illness. There was a crazy person down the street, and maybe somebody at school who wasn't quite all there. So we called him retarded or crazy. We didn't have the knowledge to understand mental illness; we just went along with what everyone said. Stigma was taught to us.

Mental illness is a journey, a path to follow. I believe that having mental illness is a journey of knowledge. I believe that my journey with mental illness has made me a better person. Without the alcohol, my vision is clearer on my journey.

Right now with my mental illness, I'm happy where I am. Being sober has added to that. I pray in the morning and ask for sobriety for the day. And if I go to bed at night and I've been sober that day I give thanks for my sobriety for the day. I went to church and had myself baptized. Because I thought if I was going to ask God to keep me sober, I had to do something for him too. So right now I'm volunteering with CMHA to give back to my community. So I'm at a good spot right now with my journey.

I understand my journey, so I can be polite to other people and understanding to them. Since I have the three virtues of compassion, empathy and patience, I can certainly give them to others.

I want to publish my poems. So there is something I want to do. I do have a book. I am also doing four plays for the London Community Players (LCP). We won at a festival and got to go into another competition with other plays. Our play started in November. It was a Christmas play, and because of the competition we went until May. That was the first time in ten years that LCP had a play in competition.

I know who I am now. I used to self-medicate because I didn't know who I was. I was living in fear. Fear is a lack of hope. Without hope, there can be no sobriety and no hope with mental illness. Think of today and hope for tomorrow.

We Have all got Some Kind of Problem: The Story of John Mackey

I got the bug for wood working in grade seven, because I was enrolled in industrial arts. I made a small tool shelf and I gave it to my parents as a present. Everything I made in grade seven I gave to my mom and my dad. I am not sure how some 40 or so years later they still had my tool shelf, but they did. So at that time I gave it to my sister's son, my nephew. I told her husband that I wanted to give it to someone special. I am glad to say that mental illness never affected my creativity because I've always been able to build stuff. Today I still do wood working.

About one week after I finished high school I started a new woodworking job at Craftsmen Circle. While there I got into a fight with this guy and when I went to work the next day my boss said the guy was not working there anymore. I was there for about six months. I got laid off because the place was going out of business. The second job I had was at Strathroy Furniture. It was the only union job I ever had, but I do not think I was there long enough to actually get into the Union. I only had that job for a couple of months and then I had my first hospitalization.

It took about one year before I got sick enough to be hospitalized. I worked through three jobs in that year. None of them worked out. I just could not keep a job.

Since I was little, I thought there was something wrong with me. My mom had this medical book and it had all kinds of diseases in it. I read it and I thought I had every disease in the book. Not just mental illness but other things. The event that made me really begin to question my mental health occurred when I was four or five years old. I had a fever and was sitting at the foot of my mom's bed. When I was sick she'd let me sleep with her. As I sat there looking at the wall next to the bed I saw these little space men crawling up the wall, with wires and hooks and stuff. They'd climb up the wall where the bumps were. It was popcorn plaster so there were a lot of bumps on the wall. Every time they missed a bump they would go back to the bottom and start all over again. But the issues with my mental health didn't come to a full-boil until I was 19 or so.

I was a quiet kid. I didn't go near people, I just kept to myself from the time I was in grade five. I was one of the new kids in the school and they treated me pretty bad because of it.

I believe my illness started from too much fighting. I had a lot of fights while I was in high school. People thought I was timid, vulnerable or scared of them, that's why they used to bug me for everything. Money, cigarettes, whatever. Or they'd try to start a fight with me over nothing. It's the way you carry yourself that I have come to believe is the important thing. It helps a lot. I got beat up a few times, but not seriously. I could always talk my way out of a fight. Keep my head up, my back straight, and my shoulders square. People would stop bugging me. I found this out through experience. I used to shrug my shoulders because my cousin did, he still does too. Last time I saw him he shrugged his shoulders. But that's the way he carries himself. I would get migraines I found by shrugging my shoulders and not keeping my back straight and my head up. Serious migraines.

It was a long time ago when I first came to Canadian Mental Health Association Middlesex (CMHA). I was sent by a psychologist at Victoria Hospital. I thought people were watching me. That's what scared me the most. That's what carried on when I was in the hospital, that people were watching me. It scared me.

Then one of the staff from CMHA put together an art-exhibit in the public library at the Cherry Hill Mall. He included some of my artwork in the exhibit and I even sold a painting. The woman who purchased the painting happened to be the superintendent of a building on Craig St. When I went over to introduce myself and to thank her for buying my work, she offered me an apartment. I went down to look at it and I said I'll take it when it is free. It was a nice little bachelor apartment. From that apartment I moved to the one I am in now. I never had to live on the streets. I've never had the nerve to do that. To ask perfect strangers for a cigarette or money. I've never had the nerve to do that. I figure people who do that must be ready to get a knuckle sandwich because if they ask somebody who's not in a good mood or something, they may look alright but if you ask them, be prepared to get a punch in the mouth just because you asked them.

I figure everybody's got some kind of problem but I don't see it as much now because I'm not a patient in the hospital. Last time I was in a hospital was 18 years ago. For me the experience was terrifying. On the very first day I was there, this old man was walking down the hall of the floor I was on in his pajama robe. As I watched him coming towards me he stopped and shook his leg. He crapped right in front of me, in that hall. I was scared to be out with the other patients. The people who were patients they used to argue and fight. You'd be sitting beside them and they'd jump up and say "what the hell did you say that for." But I didn't say anything. You know that was pretty terrifying and I hated it. I hated it from the first day I got there to the last day I was there. That time I was in the hospital for maybe 6 months. The longest I've been in hospital was 1 year.

I was diagnosed with paranoid schizophrenia. The first drug I was on, they gave to me through an injection. I felt worse after the injection than I've felt in my entire life. I felt worse on that stuff than I did before I was ever diagnosed or hospitalized or anything. But that is just my experience with going to the hospital, sometimes I will feel worse than when I go in. After that first hospital stay and when I was released I felt great. But that feeling only lasted for a couple of days, and then I was back in hospital. I think that was because of the person I was hanging around with at the time. He and I would smoke pot and drink too much. After a couple of days of that I became ill again. I was so stressed out and scared and everything. You get sucked in to that way of life, doing drugs, drinking, stealing, and fighting. And I don't want that kind of life, that's not a life for me. I don't like it so. So I just made sure to stay away.

Here is the thing, I had to accept myself as I was and stop self-medicating. When I first became ill with mental health issues I was totally in denial. I said "it can't be, you've got to be wrong. I can't be that. There's no way. You've made a mistake." Some people from the church I was attending at the time encouraged my denial. They said "oh you don't have to take medication we'll put our hands on you and pray." I didn't think that would work. I've known people even at my church that have mental illness, not necessarily the same as mine but still a mental illness.

For me it's a thing of the past. The only thing I do is take medication at night, and that's all mental illness means to me, just taking medication that's it.

Today I don't see as many patients as I would back then. There's still people at the hospital who ask me if I'm in or not. I say no, am I supposed to be in or something? It's still scary for me. Just to go to the hospital to get my blood work done; it's still scary. I'm just glad I'm not in the hospital anymore. I know the rules have changed, especially about smoking and stuff. So I'm glad I'm not in there. I can't live by those rules. It took me 20 years to stop hurting myself and another 20 years to finally stop hating myself.

In high school, there was a movie called One Flew Over the Cuckoo's Nest. When it came out I was old enough to go and see it, but I didn't go. I knew it would scare me. A bunch of kids from my school's health class took a tour of what was then called the London Psychiatric Hospital (LPH). I never went to it but I had a friend who did. When he came back he was poking fun at the people who were sick and in the LPH. My idea of mental illness stemmed from those kind-of descriptions of what the patients were like and how they would act when ill. It scared me. And then I ended up with the illness which terrified me the most and had to stay in the hospital because of it.

I'm alright now I guess. My mother died last Monday. I was afraid I would get sick again. For the first week after her passing I felt bad. It reminded me of those periods I would have when she was still alive. I'd just stare at something like the TV or anywhere else and I think I've done this before and I feel sick to my stomach. I have realized though I was more likely to get angry about something when she was alive because I was feeling her pain. But the feeling would go away in a few minutes so I did take it seriously and have managed my mental health well.

Today I don't worry too much. I have decided that if people don't want to accept me for who I am, then I have no power over that. I have no power over what they say or think of me. Today I don't take any of them too seriously.

A Better Point in Life: The Story of Jonathon Roulston

My name is Jonathon Roulston, and in November I will be 29. This year I will have been married to my wife, Tina, for nine years, and we have two healthy active children. I was born in Ingersoll, raised until grade seven in Woodstock, and from grade eight through high school we lived in Zurich Ontario.

My story of mental illness starts shortly after high school (if not earlier). In the first ten years after high school I had 12 different jobs, and had to move ten different times. The instability, along with other stressors in my life, all contributed to my depression. Because of the drawn out period of time where my depression came on I didn't even notice that anything was wrong... At least until I started having suicidal thoughts.

When that started I spoke to my doctor. And soon thereafter I was hospitalized in the Goderich psychiatric ward for the two weeks program they ran there. While in the hospital I was diagnosed with depression. At the end of the two weeks I was still feeling suicidal, and I expressed this to my doctor, but he felt that it was best for me to be discharged and get back out to be with my family. I was sent out from the hospital with the instructions to get out in the sun, do some activities that I liked, and go to the counselling sessions that were set up for me.

Despite my misgivings about this plan, I went back home. Doing what was asked of me, the next day I went out fishing (something I like, and is out in the sun). When I was fishing, I had a panic attack (or at least I wasn't thinking correctly) and I attempted to kill myself. I don't remember much for the few hours after that, but I do remember being brought back to the hospital by a police officer. So I spent another two weeks going through the program again.

When I was finally discharged the second time I was better off. I was feeling more in control of the suicidal thoughts, and was able to cope when I was out of the hospital. I then spent the next few years (and still am) going to my counsellor and working through a Cognitive Behaviour Therapy (CBT) program. I was able to stay out of the hospital and manage my depression until earlier in the year 2015. After a change in my medications I was having thoughts of self-harm and was hospitalized again for two weeks while the medications were changed again.

My depression has had a major impact on my life. It has strained my relationships: familial, fraternal, professional, and romantic. I have had trouble keeping jobs, because of the lack of motivation to get out of bed; and also the stigma associated with depression and mental illness in general. I was always afraid to tell employers about my depression because of the fear of being treated differently, and/or losing my job.

Another major impact that my depression and hospitalization caused in me, is my desire to help others. After going through the experience of trying to kill myself, and later harm myself, I don't want anyone to have to experience those things for themselves. I joined a Help/Advice forum and do everything in my power to help others through crisis situations so they don't have to feel the things I did.

Even though I have had a couple of hospitalizations, even though I have struggled with maintaining employment, even though I have a mental illness, I have still been able to find meaning in my life.

I have been able to help an untold number of people through crises and bring them to a better point in their lives.

I hope that when others with mental illness read my story, that they will find something common to their own situations, and see that despite having a mental illness they can succeed and find meaning in their own life.

We Are Not Alone: The Story of Keri Dawson

Mental illness impacted my life from the very beginning. My earliest memory is as a five-year-old. My kindergarten teacher couldn't put her finger on it but she communicated her feeling to my mother. I spent most of my childhood in the Children's Psychiatric Institute. I believe I had alcohol fetal syndrome, which makes me different from other people.

I was put back once in grade five. Later, at Forest City High School, I was put back twice for grade 12. My mother had to quit her job because I was suspended periodically and finally sent home.

My mother drank and still drinks. My mother's alcoholism made her negative to the extreme. Her negativity made me shrivel up in a corner for weeks at a time. My older brother, who is a year older than me; tried to do something about my mother's drinking, to no avail. My brother has always been very supportive. He has taken care of me since we were kids. He's my touchstone.

As I got older I used alcohol to self-medicate. After binging on alcohol I would wake up angry, and have violent outbursts, as well as periods of depression. I tried to keep it under control because ultimately only I am in control of my temperament. I still have a very hard time trying to control my moods. It doesn't happen overnight and there are quite a few distractions.

When I was first diagnosed with a mood disorder I thought mental illness was a disease. I have had many suicidal thoughts. When I first tried suicide by overdosing I was admitted to South Street Hospital for a time. Subsequently, I was admitted to the seventh floor at Victoria Hospital for psychiatric treatment. Being in the hospital scared me. I believe it made my troubles worse. Now I am just trying to cope. I still struggle to be an average person, which I guess means having flexibility of mind.

I am the only member of my family who has been diagnosed with a mental illness, so of course I stick out somewhat. I experience lows of depression but I fight to come out of them with proper treatment. It is tough because I can never stop taking the psychiatric medication that has been prescribed. There is only treatment, no cure.

I have definitely experienced discrimination because I have a mental illness. I suppose my mood disorder makes me different. I am definitely affected by my mother's alcoholism and my own. All that has happened to me is my own journey, past and present.

Accepting the fact that I have a mental illness is very hard for me; sometimes I have more difficulty than at other times. Obviously when I feel stronger I can level out and do more; I can cope with things. Still, I have to go over and over things to sort them out in my head. If I step outside of myself and look, I see an average person who has struggled with mental abuse. Mental abuse is the filter I see things through, and most of the time I feel labelled. No one can see my mental illness by looking at me, but feeling labelled still hurts.

I am trying to process all of this. This is my ongoing goal on this journey of trying to control my moods and to recover with my medication. The Canadian Mental Health Association (CMHA) has been a tremendous help. I'm supported and accepted through programs and socialization at CMHA. It has been an encouraging and significant part of my recovery. It definitely fills a big need.

I believe my story can help others. If people have similar symptoms to my own, they may think "Oh yah, she has this and that," and not feel so all alone. There are people out there who are similar, if not exactly like the rest of us. They may be in the beginning stages, or more advanced in their recovery. Try to get over the hump and it may not be that bad. We are just people after all, but more important we all deserve respect. I have found through different treatments and different groups that talking about mental illness is a positive experience that helps me to cope.

A Different Experience:
The Story of Kristeen

Through my
mental health journey,
I've had a lot of ups and
downs. I was diagnosed
with schizophrenia in
2001, after experiencing
hallucinations where I
saw many eyes and
bizarre things on walls;
I heard tons of books

slamming and slamming, driving me mad. Voices from big lips
coming at my face and especially my eyes. It was extremely
frightening. Some new mental landscape for sure.

As well as hallucinations I was extremely paranoid. Fearful like I'd
never been in my life. Everything in my life had changed. It has not
been an easy road.

I know that I am not alone. I am not the only person in the world
who goes through this. A third of people who are dealing with
schizophrenia recover, one third battle it and show improvement,
and one third never get better. I have started to improve, little by
little. I am staring to feel better thank goodness.

I really did not know what to expect from my hospitalization. When
I thought of it I envisioned a place where all the patients were
restrained. Very frightening. Today I am more relaxed about the
hospital because I now know the reality. Sometimes there is
craziness on the other side. People think bad things about therapy
and counselling or psychologists and psychiatrists, but those same
professionals have really helped me manage my life today.

All the staff were very cordial to me while I was in hospital. Of
course the nurses knew I was deaf, and would make sure I had
enough food and regulated me to bathe, and so on. Still I never got

used to being in a mental health hospital. Hospitals were almost second nature to me because prior to my mental health crisis I'd had heart surgery, as well as eye surgery, which were in other hospital locations. Those stays were fast: in and out. But living in a mental health institute was a different experience all together.

While I was being observed the psychiatrist came to see me every day with a sign language interpreter. All his questions led to a lot of very good discussions and conversations. He was the one who would diagnosed me with schizophrenia.

Being the only deaf person there amongst all the others, I had no real communication. Still, I was feeling like I had a somewhat new and positive outlook. While in hospital I enjoyed communicating through crafts. I made things, painted, drew, wrote-free-expression. I liked being creative in the hospital. It was something solid, grounding. It made me feel better, something I could control.

I saw many different people while I stayed in hospital with many different diagnoses. I was frightened by them all. I wanted to escape from the hospital, to jump out of the window, and just go. I felt there was too much pressure on me. It was not long until I was thinking about suicide. My mind was all over the place. Even the doctors were afraid I was going to kill myself. I did not communicate much.

When I did try to suicide my goal was simply to get away from all my mental health issues. I wanted my suffering to end it. All the doctors and staff who were caring for me really helped. They made me see it is not the end of the world – not really. They worked tirelessly to help me feel more positive, that suicide was not the answer. They gave me proper medication and combined it with counselling and therapy. They encouraged me that I would start feeling better soon. It's true, now that I am beginning to have a better understanding of what schizophrenia is and mental health overall.

Around 60% of schizophrenics attempt suicide at least once in their lives. After having those feelings, I stayed in the hospital for a month. I was by myself. I was the only deaf person there.

Today I now know a hospital is a safe place for me. Everyone there is helpful. Educating my friends and family who believe I am just crazy. They were uncomfortable around me because they didn't think I was the same person as I was before. Sometimes I do have hallucinations and I hear stuff inside my head. So my behavior changes from the stress of what I am dealing with.

Getting on the right medication was also hard and took a long time to get right. Sometimes one pill would help but then they would find out that with that type of pill I was gaining too much weight or it was causing a great deal of confusion. Then they would give me some new pills, and maybe that one wasn't enough. So they started to add more, hence I would have to take them more frequently throughout the day. I would have to take pills four or five times a day to help manage the symptoms. But that was before. Today, all my medication is delivered in an injection.

My family and friends felt the impacted of my illness. My family didn't even know what was wrong with me because I hadn't told them I had symptoms until about a year ago. Finally I told my sister, and she understood. So she knew. My sister and I had a conversation, and she asked about my medications. Plus we had a discussion about counselling. She understood because she had mental health issues around depression. And yes, I have depression too.

People at my church also helped me. When my symptoms were much worse, I couldn't go to church for a long time and so the pastor came to visit me. He encouraged me not to be afraid to go to church. It doesn't matter who you are and what you're struggling with. Everyone there will be supportive, accepting, and understanding. He told me that they would learn from me and that they would support me with prayers. The people there have been very supportive, and I do feel much, much better now.

My friends were absolutely shocked that I had schizophrenia. I had hid it from them all. When my symptoms were acting up I would stay home. That way my friends never saw me at times when I was unwell. The result was my own friends didn't know me as a person who struggled with mental illness. My friends slowly started to comprehend my condition when I started to talk to them about it. I didn't want to hide anymore. I wanted to express how I was feeling, and what was really going on with me.

Last June I told my mom about how I read some magazines pamphlets about schizophrenia. My mom said, "I don't want to hear about that trash".

I wanted so badly to tell her about what I was going through. I wanted her to understand more about me, and to share my experience about myself and what other people were going through. My mom wouldn't hear it, she didn't want anything to do with it. But my sister, she helped.

When I got my diagnosis of schizophrenia I felt stunned. I thought, "That word." I had never heard that word attached to me before.

"I have schizophrenia." The diagnosis frightened me so much.

In that moment my life changed forever.

I feel there is stigma. Schizophrenia is awful – it is an awful word to be labelled with.

I feel there is stigma which the individual with mental health issues has to contend with. Some people with mental health issues are suicidal. That was a part of my past as well. People can't always control their actions especially when they are not well.

I never self-medicated or abused anyone. However, I might completely upset a room, trying to destroy things could make me feel better. Then I would clean the room; that would help my highly emotional mind calm down.

I lost my job because of this mental illness. I just couldn't handle it, it was very hard for me to concentrate on work and I was feeling paranoid, which was causing a lot of problems at work. Generally some people couldn't stand to be with me because of the hallucinations. Even though I was fortunate and happy working there because I had made a few friends at work who did understand and support me.

I know it is hard but even though you are dealing with mental health issues try to stay positive, so you can open yourself to God and develop strong and supportive friends who are willing to listen and assist. Don't hide yourself from people, you don't want to wear a mask. There are good counsellors and nurses that can help you.

I like to go to programs as they help me stay positive and not think about suicide or become negative. My counsellor comes to visit me at home and we talk and I receive support and encouragement to go out and do different things. I feel good because I am improving.

To stay positive I talk to God and write in a journal every day. I try to smile, and be nice to myself. Now that my family and friends understand me a bit better, I am more at ease.

We are Just People: The Story of Lexi Vienneau

Nobody really understands mental illness because it's such a broad term. You hear mental illness and you don't know if someone is dealing with depression or dissociative identity disorder until you really talk to them. People just sort of assume things about each other.

Mental illness impacts every single facet of my life. Like going to school, which is just something everyone is supposed to do, but for me it is difficult. And how about getting up and having conversations with my own family, I just didn't have the energy.

I had my first panic attack when I was 12 and at the time my family and I had no idea what was going on. We were in the car and we had just gotten on the 401 highway to go to Toronto. I didn't feel well, my stomach hurt, I was sitting in the back of the car crying and of course my parents were like "You have a stomach ache, be quiet. We already paid." We were going to Cirque Du Soliel and so they were; "we are just going." I didn't care about what we were going to do. I just needed to not be in that car at that time. I needed us to get off the highway and go home.

I was 14 years old when I was diagnosed. Still pretty young. At the time I thought if someone has a mental illness they were crazy. Even today there are not always realistic representations of someone dealing with mental health issues. So I thought to have a mental illness was to be crazy. And that a person who was crazy just sat on the street talking to themselves and had pet squirrels. Back then I believed you stayed away from anyone with a mental illness.

At one point my anxiety got really bad. My parents found an inpatient program I could attend. I was to go there for three months. But, my anxiety was so bad that they actually couldn't get me to go. It was a program where you could not be forced into it, a voluntary program. I never made it to that program. It would have been really good for me but I just couldn't do it.

I remember it was so frustrating not being able to articulate what was happening to me. A couple weeks before high school, I stopped going out. I wouldn't talk to my friends. I just stopped doing everything. I wouldn't leave my bedroom. The night before the first day of my first year of high school I was hyperventilating. It was late at night so I knocked on my parents doors, three or four times. Through the door I said, "Please wake up, I know it's the middle of the night but I can't go to school in the morning." At that point, they didn't know anything about mental illness, I didn't know anything. They told me to "Shut up and go to sleep. Of course you have to go to school in the morning."

The next day I went to school and had a horrible panic attack in the middle of class. I got really dizzy, I couldn't stand, I went to the nurse's office and my mom came to pick me up. That was when we were like there is something really wrong with me.

So we made a doctor's appointment. They did everything. CAT scans, blood work, all sorts of things. They couldn't find anything wrong with me. My doctor finally suggested a therapist. Just to talk to. I went to the therapist. It was my therapist who said "Sounds like you're dealing with anxiety."

That started my long journey. It took time to understand what anxiety is and what it actually means. I started on some medications but I would not always take them. I was 14 years old and I just want to be like everyone else. I think it took me a couple of years to really start telling people "This is why I can't do things." I used to lie if I didn't want to go somewhere, I'd just tell people I was sick because I didn't want people to know there was anything wrong with me.

I know my illness was hard for my mom, my stepdad, and brother. When you're dealing with your own mental illness you don't think a lot about how you are affecting the people who love you. You can't care. They're not the ones with the illness. I was the one who needs help. But I now know you need to care how the people you love feel. It is interesting now that I don't live at home, we talk more. I have learned it was really difficult for my mom. My illness took a toll on her financially. She had to pay for help and medication. She wanted so badly for me to be happy. I don't think I realized how painful it was for my mom to have to watch me struggle so much just to do everyday things.

My mom would have to come wake me up in the mornings and sometimes beg me to get out of bed. I think that must have been really painful for her; to just want her child to feel good but I was unable to. My family would go on trips and I would refuse to go. They wanted the trip to be a family experience but that would not happen.

My brother has never been talkative, but I could tell he did what he could and he was always there for me. For instance if we were going somewhere and suddenly I would have a panic attack he would pass me his game boy or he'd tell my parents that we have to stop. We don't talk about what's wrong with me.

When I was 16 years old I transferred schools and so the whole going to school process started again. That's when I finally decided if I'm ever going to have friends, I have to just be honest with people and tell them this is what I am dealing with. It did take me a while but I did finally come to terms with that. My mental health issues are a part of who I am. And that's okay.

I didn't have a boyfriend until I was 20. He's really great. His family are really religious. So when he and I started dating we had to follow their rules. No unsupervised dates, no living together before marriage, and we shouldn't kiss before we get married.

We had been together for about five or six months when I had a really horrible panic attack. I was house sitting at the time out in the country on a farm. I was by myself with six dogs. I was really freaking out. So I called my boyfriend because I wanted him to come out to the farm. It was in the middle of winter and he was busy. He told me he could not drive out to the farm to help me. I sort of lost it on him and was like "What do you mean you won't come see me?!"

After that incident his parents tried to have me committed because they said I was a crazy person. They said "We're going to call 911 and have you taken into the hospital because you're going kill yourself or hurt our son." It was awful, my boyfriend and I talked it through and we decided it was something we could move past. He knew all about my anxiety issues. He didn't really think it was a big deal but I guess his family did and after that they started to harass me, a lot.

My boyfriend and I moved out together. At the time his phone was still on a family plan. His family went through his phone records and got my phone number. They would text me and call me. Especially his sister. They would say really awful and hurtful things. They told me I shouldn't be with their son. They said, "You're just going to kill yourself anyways so why would you want to put him through that." It was really horrific and stressful to say the least. At one point his brother showed up at our house in his big pickup truck and purposefully tore up our gravel drive. It was just really horrible. My boyfriend and I ended up moving again so that his family wouldn't know where we lived. And I changed my phone number to end the harassing calls. It was a nightmare. It has been many years since we have had contact with them.

I've met so many different people throughout my life that have had different mental illnesses. They are all so different and you can't tell by looking at someone that they are dealing with mental health issues. So I've just come to realize that it doesn't look like anything, we are all just people.

I don't think you're ever really recovered from mental illness. You just learn how to manage it. It is mostly a journey of acceptance. It will always be a part of my life. I will always have panic attacks and that is okay. I know that sometimes I'm still going to feel depressed and I know I'm going to get through it. I've come to terms with that and know that it's okay. It's alright if you're not happy all the time. No one is really happy all the time. This life is a journey and I would say I am still on my way. But I think I've passed the half-way point (if there is such a thing).

I think anybody's story of lived experience can help. It shows people that they are not the only one who is dealing with a mental illness. When I was first dealing with anxiety I thought I was the only person in the world that this is happening to. I read some books, went online, and found out lots and lots of people are dealing with this. Just that helped me a lot, knowing you're not the only one. No matter what your story is. I think it just helps build a sense of community. And then you can overcome.

Acceptance : The Story
of Linda Black

I'm a slower person and
a slower person has to
work harder than another
person.

School was hard for me
due to my unique
learning style. I had to
fight my way through
the school system. I
went both to an
opportunity school and a
regular school.

I learned at an early age that I had to do things differently because I
was taught differently. Once I was in school I found out fast that there is
prejudice. They just did not understand and so they discriminated. They
use to say names and stuff like that, you know, like you're stupid,
you're retarded.

In my grade nine year I was first placed in a grade nine class for
individuals who were slow. And then they switched me and placed
me in the regular grade nine class. So the way I see it I was too smart
to be in an alternative school and I was too dumb to make it in
regular school.

I developed mental health issues while in school. The kids at school
were hard on me. They always made fun of me because I was
different than they were. Today schools do not tolerate that kind of
bullying but back when I was in school teachers stayed out of it. As
a result, I faced the bulling daily and it wore me down. Then to add
to my struggles I found it hard to deal with people.

I had a hospitalization in 2009 and I stayed for about a month. I was at my friend's house just hanging out. I do not know why it happened but by the time I got home I was doing crazy things. My boyfriend said, "You're going to the hospital." So I went to the hospital. That was it.

I remember I was so frightened. I was afraid to leave my apartment. I began to see hallucinations. I was terrified to go to the hospital for mental health issues because I had heard some awful stories about what happened to people when they did. I was sure I would be in there for a long time. The way a hospital stay for mental illness was portrayed on TV, I imagined it would be like that.

When I was diagnosed with a mental illness I not only had to deal with hallucinations but I also could hear voices in my head. It was so scary. I believed that once I heard voices, the doctors would classify me as a mental-case and that I would never recover. But that is not the case.

In time I accepted that I had mental health issues and began to look after myself. My medication began to work and I started going to CMHA. I went to the classes that they offered and that helped me to recover.

Today I go to CMHA and they're really good there. The way I see it if I hadn't had them I would have probably went back into the hospital. My recovery is better managed when I have the professional support. So I just take my pills the way I'm supposed to and go to different groups and I'm OK.

I take one day at a time. I just had three teeth extracted about three weeks ago. I still have five more to go. I hope this helps different people and that my story was positive and that's it. I feel pretty good now. That's what recovery is all about.

Close to the Edge:
The Story of
Patricia Penny Dale
(Penny)

People kept telling
me that I had
problems. But I
lived my life close
to the edge, so
problems were kind
of how I coped.

At nine years of age I was taken from my family. My mother was
dealing with addictions and we did not have help. No one did back in
the 1960s, you just did the best you could. My father was able to
look after some of my brothers and sisters, but I was too much of a
handful, and so I went into foster care for a bit. After two months, he
was awarded custody of me and so my father raised me and my
siblings on his own.

By the time I was twelve years of age my mental illness began to
surface. At the time I was in a court- ordered training school. I hated
it there as you can imagine and wanted to get back home. I cut my
arms with the expectation that I would be allowed to return to my
family home. It did not work, the Psychiatrist I had at the time
decided the London Psychiatric Hospital was the best place for me.
She ordered that I receive many drugs to calm me down and off I
went. To this day I cannot remember my first days in that hospital.
So my first admittance happened in 1969 at 12 years of age. I have
had many more since then.

During my first hospital stay I did not really understand that acting
out did not serve me well. I thought I would be allowed to just do my
own thing, but that was not the case. The nurses and doctors showed
me: when I would act out or refuse to do something they would drug

me and place me in solitary confinement. Back in those days, it was not so easy to get out.

The first time I was in solitary, I was in there for a week. They did not give me a bed, just a blanket but no pillow. I had to sleep on the floor. The next time I was placed in solitary it was for the same reason. I tried to run away from the hospital. They caught me, and put me in seclusion for three months. They wanted to show me enough was enough.

I always hated it when they gave me medication. I never knew what they were giving me and so I would refuse to take it. The nurses would try to convince me it was for my wellbeing but I did not believe them, and would refuse. This meant they would give me the medications by injections, whether I agreed or not. It always seemed they would shoot me up with medications and when I would come-to I would once again be in seclusion. It took me a while to remember that I was not in charge of my care, they were.

I lived in and out of psychiatric hospitals for many years, but I guess the one which left the deepest impression was when I was 19 years of age. It was 1977 and my mom had died a few weeks before. Though I had not had a simple relationship with my mother, I still loved her deeply. Her death coincided with the birth of my first daughter. I did not, handle either very well.

My mom's passing destroyed me. The psychiatrist I was seeing told me it was crazy for me to love her so, as she had been a terrible mother. But that was not the point: she was my mother. So I told him firmly we would no longer discuss my mother. I do not remember much for many of the months after her passing. But when my memory returned I was in the Forensic Psychiatric Hospital (FPH) in St Thomas.

To this day I am not sure how or why they decided the FPH was where I needed to be. I had not had any involvement with the law.

I went missing for a while and was discovered living in Toronto. I understand from my family that I was admitted in that city to the

Queen Street Mental Health Center (now called Center for Addictions and Mental Health). Then for some reason they sent me to St Thomas' FPH. Though the place looked like other hospitals I had been in, there was one main difference: all day long I was kept in straps (shackles) on both my hands and feet. They left deep cuts and hurt. If they decided you needed to be punished in some way they would order you on your knees, and you would stay in that position for sometimes hours.

The FPH also did not allow us to just hang around; we had to attend programs throughout our day.Of course we did the groups in our straps. Still they helped me to learn about myself, which I really needed. I realized I was aggressive and had many walls built around myself. Today I still deal with this but I am managing better.

Things settled down a lot in 2003, when I finally got into CMHA Housing. I had been to the Queen's Avenue site of CMHA many times, and I would feel nervous and run away. Then I took a friend with me to ease my nerves. I realized it was not so bad there. So I stuck around and stopped running away.

Today, I live in a nice home with nice neighbours who I often visit with. I realize that for me to get help with my mental illness I have to really want the help. I mean you have to want it really deep inside yourself. Now I have made some close friendships. My best friend also deals with mental health issues. She taught me to put my eye where the ball is if I want to catch it. Today I am proud of myself as I am finally living a life not so close to edge.

Beginning Physicality Resolve: The Story of Richard Barton

My first experience with prejudice and discrimination was in school: I was called names, harassed and looked upon as an outsider. I never had many friends. Nobody wanted to be around me. I had a seizure disorder, and everyone thought I was mentally challenged. My seizures, the way I walked, the way I talked, my tone of voice, all gave people the impression I was mad. I am sure that there are people out there who know who I am today. There is not as much prejudice and discrimination today. My family and friends cope, and deal with my mental illness the best that they can.

At first I did not want to have a mental illness. I suppose nobody does. I didn't want it to be true so I tried not to believe it. But that was just for a short period of time. I began to accept my situation. However, I lacked motivation and found it hard to figure out what to do. I could not see what was out there for me to do. This period of time was one of the hardest for me to endure. In time my commitment to my recovery and my heath finally showed me the way to recovery.

Before anyone told me that I have a mental health illness, I was always self-diagnosing. I was always reading up on medical conditions. I educated myself on all of my conditions, both physical and emotional. I approached my doctors with what I had researched and they looked into what I had shared with them. I felt involved in my care but was worried that maybe the doctors were not as well informed as they could be, not even a doctor in Sarnia who followed me to make sure I was alright. So I moved to London because I believed there would be doctors with more current ideas.

Moving to London did help me, though it took some time. Now I can see as many doctors as I need. When I go to the hospital I feel confident that they go over what I am talking about, making sure that everything is alright.

It is my opinion that we all have a form of mental illness. It is just that some people have it more severe than others. I spent four years in the hospital due to my mental illness. At first I had a great deal of trouble fitting into the hospital routine. But in time I managed to settle in. I was allowed to leave the hospital on a pass, and so I went shopping at the local mall, just to get a coffee and goodies for myself and the other patients. I picked up something for the staff if they wanted it as well. I used this time and took the opportunity to help others. Still, it was such a long stay in hospital.

Going through the hospitalization brought me back to my school years, to people I once knew. It was like my past was happening again and people were tormenting me. Somehow the hospital surroundings helped me to get over these memories, and ultimately helped my health, stability, balance, and moods. Through the help and guidance of my new doctors, my physical and mental health has improved beyond expectations. I am back on track now, back on my feet, living in the community.

For years I was unstable because of the seizures, because of the continuing unbalance of both my mind and body. Over the past five years I have come through a lot of what troubled me. I am now on a steady and balanced regiment of medications allowing me to be on a daily routine. At last I am out, flowing with the traffic of people that surround me. I feel now as though I am not afraid to do anything.

Now I have many positive experiences. I feel that I am living the best part of my life's journey. Through the local Canadian Mental Health Association (CMHA) I am around people every day, not just sitting around and watching the television. I have the motivation to be around people and friends. I socialize, and communicate with people now like never before. It definitely helps to improve my health and self-care through positive interactions.

Baby Steps and Knocking Down Barriers: The Story of Robert Chatterson

My journey with obsessive compulsive disorder (OCD) began when my kidneys failed. That event would hospitalize me for eight days at the London Health Sciences Center (LHSC). When I came home my doctor, who cared for me for ten years, discovered I needed prostate surgery. I was admitted to Strathroy Hospital for that. I was in there for four days. These two events caused me too much stress.

At the same time, my wife Jeanie's health started to change. She was taking diabetic medication, and not really watching her diet or her numbers. As a result, she had to use insulin to manage her illness. She relied on me to administer two needles every night. With my OCD, my anxiety peaked. My biggest fear was I would hit a vein and she would bleed out. Once I got over that fear and saw that I could administer the needle properly, I calmed down.

At the same time I was struggling at work. I was a chef at one of the senior's homes in the city of London. I was falling behind on my work because I was going back and double checking things. Work soon noticed. My wife noticed about a year before that. Something was changing with me. I also knew something was changing because I was double-checking a lot of stuff. I rechecked the stoves, checked the fans, asked Jeanie to check things as well. I asked people to check things because it made me secure that someone else had also checked, so it must be alright.

So on 27 March 2007, I went to work, chef jacket on, chef hat, walked onto the middle of the floor in my cooking area, and just stood frozen. I could not move. I just stopped. My co-workers, the cooks, took me by my arms and helped me into the supervisor's office. I was able to drive back to Strathroy. My wife called her sister and said to her that we had to go to the emergency room. That's when I was admitted to LHSC, and later diagnosed with OCD.

At around 11:30pm they transferred me from LHSC to the Old South Hospital. I stayed on the 8th floor for about 14 days for observation and assessment. I had my own room and everything was provided. My wife came in from Strathroy to see me. She came one day and then skipped a day because that's a long way to drive. I would not shave until she arrived.

If you ever watch the movie One Flew Over the Cuckoo's Nest starring Jack Nicholson, I went through the same thing. We walked the walls, and we held the railings. We lined up for our pills, and put our tongues out for the nurses to check to see that we were not hiding them. When my food came, I detailed the items on my tray. I counted everything, and then went back and counted again. I used to put my tray on the wagon, go back to check that it was still there, and confirm that I had indeed put it on the wagon. Stuff like that.

I was allowed to come home for a couple of days but then it was straight back to the hospital. They had put me on the 7th Floor by then. The medicine that was prescribed for me started to kick in a little bit.

I started a 15-week Cognitive Behavioural Therapy (CBT) course, which was excellent. I also saw my family doctor and was involved in a program in Strathroy's Canadian Mental Health Association (CMHA) Middlesex site. I had my therapist appointments at the LHSC. He is an OCD specialist. I've been seeing him since 2007. He has brought me a long way. I had many charts. I broke down my illness and created charts with detailed information. It seemed logical. But my doctor said, "Robert, I have never seen anyone include so much detail." My response was, "I don't need a computer, my computer is right here in my head."

I had 24 columns: check fridge, check oven, check toaster, check dryer, check washer, and so on. It was a compulsive drive within me to check all these things. Or I'd ask my wife Jeanie to do it. Over the years, we slowly got the numbers less and less. We're down to four now. We are still working to reduce the numbers.

My number one issue is contamination. In medical terms this is called germ phobia. I'm still dealing with that.

I had a second hospital stay. While there I took programs, like arts and that kind of stuff. I did better during that stay because I had different nurses. I even had a male nurse. He said to me one day, "Robert here's your blade, here's your shaving cream, the washroom's right there. I'll come back in 10 minutes and check on you. Okay." So I shaved in the bathroom, which was in the bedroom. When the nurse returned, I was just finishing up. He took the shaving cream and the razor blade, and I was fine from then on. It was a barrier that we just broke. This was great because when my wife came, we could have that extra hour to spend together because before she would watch me while I shaved. So that was a barrier that we broke. That has been the theme for me since the year 2000. It's all about breaking the barriers. So that's what we did. Slowly.

I didn't operate at all the first year I was diagnosed. I did nothing in the kitchen. I couldn't even go near my home kitchen. My wife Jeanie was a tower of strength. She did everything. I would sit at the kitchen table and she would say, "Undo your hands."

I would hold on to the table. As long as I grabbed something tightly then I wouldn't do something that might hurt somebody. It was almost a safety procedure for me. I wanted everyone to be safe around me. I wanted everything to be safe. I literally would follow my wife around our house. I was her shadow.

I felt safe as long as I was with Jeanie and we were in the house. That was my comfort zone. Jeanie would have some peace of mind around nine at night. That's when she gave me my heavier meds, and they just knocked me out. That's the only time of the day that peace would take my soul and I could rest. When I woke up at eight in the morning it would just start all over again.

It has been medically proven that the onset of OCD occurs later in life. My mother has it, my uncle has it, and my youngest sister has it. It's very treatable. My medicine took about seven weeks to kick in and I still take them every day. They're precious because for the longest time I was in darkness.

I have recorded a CD of songs I have written. As I write on my CD, "Out of the Darkness into the Light", the darkness is the tunnel, but I knew I had to stay in the tunnel to find Robert and bring him home. I would say to my wife. I've got to go away dear, but I will bring Robert home to you. That was me telling her, I'll probably be hospitalized. I could feel the time was coming.

Eventually that is what would happen. I would be hospitalized. But I knew I would have to stay in the tunnel because at the end of the tunnel there's a light. But I didn't know where I was, I kind of lost myself.

Christmas 2009 was on a Friday. We spent Christmas together with my step-son and his daughter. On the Sunday night, at about 9:15, we were all watching TV. I took our dog Lilly outside. I wasn't gone longer than three minutes. My wife Jeanie went upstairs and while climbing the stairs lost her balance and fell backwards. She broke a blood vessel in her brain. She needed to be rushed to Strathroy Hospital and then they transferred her to LHSC.

When I found her at the bottom of the stairs she was in a pool of blood. There was so much blood, I found it hard to think. I heard the ambulance, I knew she was already going to heaven. Because I called 911 with horror and fear in my voice, they told me what to do. I went with the towels, and put my hands on her head. My hands were full of her blood. Two ambulances and the police came to the house.

My mind began to play tricks on me and my thoughts raced. I couldn't understand because, to me, it seemed like around the corner there was a church pew. There were two officers who were sitting in the church pew. I got up to see what was going on. So much commotion. It looked like bags were flying all around. I heard the pumping of the oxygen. The officer kept telling me to please sit down. I cried and wanted to see my wife, but the officer warned me that it was important that I sit down.

I couldn't put this awful situation together in my mind. I looked at the officer and said; "Who do you think touched her? Who do you think helped her? Who do you think put those towels there?"

If you ever watch crime shows on television and see where they mark out where the body laid, and spread the area with the fake blood, well, I had the real thing. When I came in from putting my dog Lilly to bed, I grabbed my coffee, was going back downstairs to watch television and there was my wife Jeanie, at the bottom of the stairs, lying in a pool of blood around her head. I knew it was fatal because there was just so much blood.

The detective who was on the case had to interview me. I was interviewed in the Strathroy Police Station. This was something they had to do and I know that. The detective was wonderful with me. I think he was a bit confused and concerned because at that point my OCD was triggered. I washed my hands so much that they began to bleed. I'd be having this interview with the detective and my hands were turning red and he'd say Robert? I told him I struggle with OCD. I was interviewed by the police for about three hours.

I would spend 2010 by myself in the house. Me and my OCD. It was a roller coaster ride. It was weeks before I could take those stairs. It was just hard facing that. But eventually I had to do laundry, so I had to. I went to the cemetery and got closure with Jeanie. I said I've got to move on with my life dear. I still visit her. Then 2011 came around, and I was determined in my soul. I said okay, this year it's you and OCD. It's going to be the two of us, and we're going to spend a lot of time together because I am going to knock down a lot of barriers.

When I had to do grocery shopping for myself, it would take me over two hours. I'd pick something off the shelf, get over to another aisle, then go back to the same one again. But I would tell myself 'you're fine Robert.' Going through the check-out I had issues.

Because I can't do anything fast, I must go from A to B. So I'd be packing my groceries and, of course, me being a chef, meat has to be packaged by itself. Chemicals like soap and laundry soap have to be packaged separately. I don't want Tide with my sliced meat, so I had bags, and I'd be taking a little longer. I thought to myself 'no OCD you're not having it your way: we're going to pack these groceries whether you like it or not.' Then I thought I would ask for help. I just asked the cashier for help. I said "I need help because I can't multitask." They are more than willing to help. I go through now and I talk with them as I pack. I got rid of that barrier. Take that OCD, and see you later. You got to take control of your life, and tomorrow is so precious. I know what I want to do tomorrow.

I met Deb in the hospital but I had known her for over 28 years. She was waiting to see the doctor and I was cleaning the hallway. I could hear someone saying "hello Bob," but it went right over my head because I go by Robert. And then she said Robert, but I still couldn't see anybody. So she was laying in bed and I walked in her room and said is that you Deb? After so many years, I found it amazing. We got together for a coffee. Then I began to call her. In time she moved into my home. After living together for a while we decided to get married.

At the time she was able to work but shortly after we married, she had a mental health crisis. She was diagnosed with four disorders. She has decided not to return to work. I'm okay with that. Together we have strength. I walk her through it. I reassure her every day. I tell her, "Look, you're important. There's only one of you in the world. You will walk again." This is a mantra that I've always said to myself: "baby steps."

That's the phrase I've always used for myself. And I said to Deb "I will show you baby steps and you will have your life back." She's at the point now with her meds, and she is being seen by a specialist. She's just getting her life back on track now, doing some volunteer work with CMHA.

I am proud of the strength that I've had. I've prayed to the Lord that I would love someone again; that for the rest of my life I could have one person to love. I look at my life and I want to live for tomorrow because I'm important, and I've still got a lot left to do in the world. Faith is important to me. In my house we have a written statement, "I'm not afraid to go because I love today." Take it Lord, take my soul. I'm here for you, your arms are open. I'm ready to come.

I got involved in volunteering at the hospital. I'm in housekeeping. It gave me back to the world. They are so supportive of me at the hospital, in the housekeeping department. They put me back in the community. It got me interacting with people. I absolutely love it. I live for it actually. I take it very seriously. I do five hour shifts, three days a week. I start at 6 a.m. or at 4 p.m. The early shift is not an issue for me. I'm a chef. For 20 years I've been up early. I always start my day at 5 a.m.

My supervisor at Strathroy hospital is in charge of housekeeping. One morning she did a miracle for me. I had an obsessive thought that I could not go into the laundry room unless she went in first. The laundry room is a big, big room. I just couldn't walk into it because it was overwhelming. The door would be closed and I wouldn't open it until people came and I would want them to turn the lights on. My supervisor knew this. Well one day she took me by the hand and as we held hands and talked, we got closer and closer to the laundry room door. I could feel my senses rising. She must have felt it in my hand. She said to me, "You're okay Robert. You're with me. I've got your hand." And we got closer to the laundry room door. I automatically just closed my eyes, and she led me towards the door. She then said "Open your eyes Robert." I said, "No dear, that's a tunnel. I don't want to go into the tunnel." She said, "No, you're fine. Open your eyes, I'm with you, I'm right here. You're okay." I opened my eyes and it was brightness.

So I did the same thing for the next four days. I went down the hall by myself. I knew there were other staff working in the hospital in case I needed help. I closed the laundry room door and as I got closer I closed my eyes and then reached in and up the wall, to hit the switch. On the fifth day I think I just walked straight in and flipped the switch and that barrier was broken.

I have four sisters and one day I was speaking to the youngest. She lives in London. She and I have had an ongoing conversation for five years. It started out small. All my sisters call me Bobby. She told me that she was checking things over and over. In time our conversations got longer and longer and I realized her compulsions were also becoming stronger. She could no longer hide them she said to me. I told her to call her doctor and to get a referral and that I would go with her to support her. She agreed.

The following week I was again speaking to her on the phone to find out if she had followed through and made a doctor's appointment. She sounded so upset and her voice was shaky. I said, "What's wrong dear?" She said, "I just have terrible thoughts. "I asked, "What are your thoughts what are you thinking about? "She said, "I want to take my life." And I said, "You stay where you are, get a glass of water, sit down and take some deep breathes. I'm coming now. I'll be there in 40 minutes."

I had my wife Deb call her every five minutes to talk to her and keep her on the line. When I got there she was crying and shaking, full of anxiety. Her bedroom door was open and there was a scarf hanging over the door. I knew she wanted to hurt herself so badly. I said, "We are going to the emergency department right now." So we went. She was diagnosed with depression and anxiety. She's stabilizing now with medication and is staying with Deb and me. She's doing really well now: she's eating and sleeping well. The family has come to see her so she has a ton of support.

I said to my sister, "Look dear, I will show you baby steps, I will show you the magic of baby steps. You will find that you will learn to love yourself again. You'll look outside and there won't be a tunnel of darkness. There will be a light. You'll run and play with your grandchildren."

I'm not afraid of tomorrow. And I enjoyed yesterday and I definitely love today. So now there is a brightness. I came out of the dark tunnel. I came home. I continue every day with OCD, my medical plans, and my therapy. And now I challenge OCD every day. I also thought, 'Okay Robert it's time to pick up the guitar again.'

I can't read music but I can play by ear. I signed up for guitar classes. I've written about 80 songs. I've also written songs for people who've experienced something in their life that's been hard for them to cope with. I write it and I give it to them. They come back and thank me. They say, "I don't know how you came up with the lyrics." It's helped them to cope and feel understood, which is good. It took me a while to understand I was not going to put my chef jacket and hat back on: that's not going to be a possibility. I accept that I cannot multitask. It is too overwhelming. I just cannot break that barrier.

Anyone from both Strathroy Hospitals is eligible to receive an award for volunteer work. I was nominated and I won. I got a beautiful watch and letter from the CEO. They had a reception at one of the golf courses, and I had the opportunity to say a few words. When they called me to receive my award they gave me the cordless microphone, so I could come from behind and go right out to the tables and talk to the people. I just told them my story. That was so special to be able to do that.

I'm in the light now but I've just got a little further to go. I do my gardening, I love gardening. I've got my vegetables and stuff. I'm also doing art work: pictures and music. I would love it if my music and pictures came together.

Literally, I am out of the darkness and in the light. My supervisor from the hospital did something for me that I will hold dear to my heart for the rest of my life. I'm just thankful for life. I'm thankful that I've been given a second chance and could help people along the way. I will continue to speak about my journey, play my music, garden, paint and volunteer.

Hitting the Wall:
The Story of Robert
Lockyear

I'm an old
school guy. I came
up when all of
today's experts were
in school learning all
the things that they
know now. The
programs we have
today to aid children
in their learning
weren't available
back then. The
government and
educational system were not up to speed. Education today is a whole
new ball game. The kids get services now. Services that I needed but
never got. As a result, my school experience was brutal. It was hell.
If I knew then what I know now, there wouldn't have been any
problems. School would have been better for me. There would have
been adjustments and accommodations made to my education. But
the reality is there wasn't.

Education was at a turning point, just at the cusp. Back then they
were still slapping kids for doing wrong, forcing kids to write with
their right hand even if they naturally wrote with their left. That is
where my story starts.

I started out as just a regular kind of kid living in the Canadian
prairies. I was born in 1957 in the province of Saskatchewan. In time
my family moved to Edmonton, Alberta. I was a tough little prairie
kid playing in the snow.

I went to a preschool run by the Grey Nuns. They were nice and they
actually figured out that I was having a little bit of trouble with my
learning. They used a lot of good materials: with pictures, and

learning letters, and teaching us how to write and print. They Grey Nuns had a lot of patience. They worked with me one on one. Back in those days that was above and beyond the acceptable practice. It was really excellent and I didn't realize how good. The style of one on one learning really was the best way for me to learn.

Back in my day the Alberta school system began with Kindergarten. They had a strict rule that only children born within a twelve month period could be enrolled. So that meant anyone having a January birthday would be the oldest in their class. My birthday is in January so I was a year behind in school. Which was tough. It felt like I had to do kindergarten twice. I felt like I did something wrong.

In grade two they began to teach the kids how to write. I wrote with my left hand and was forced to use my right hand. They were really stuck on that. It was not easy for me but I did learn how to be a little bit ambidextrous over time.

In time my family moved from Alberta to British Columbia (BC). I was older and worked hard to fit in with kids. I was the new kid in town so to them I was a bit odd. I spent a lot of time at Stanley Park, and learned a lot at the Zoo and on the beaches. We would go to White Rock and mess around putting pennies on the rails of the train track. I got into Cubs Scouts and the Boy Scouts. It was a big thing.

Grade 5 and 6 there was an ex-royal navy officer who was the vice principal at my school. He saw I was being bullied by the other kids and separated me out and helped me out of the trouble I was having. At the same school I was tested for learning disabilities. I was diagnosed with perceptual problems. But my comprehension in reading, and my verbal skills were high, so that kind of fooled them.

I aggravated my grade eight teacher. She worked hard to teach me grammar. I tried so hard but I was just not getting it. She would not give it up and what happened is I became more and more self-conscious. School was not easy for me. It made me awkward in social situations. I was lucky to have a family that supported me. Helped me to learn in ways other than school.

As a kid the best way for me to learn was through experience. I have been lucky enough to do some travelling and to learn a lot about the planet. In my family, summer was all about travelling. Summer trips were called dad's tours. It was fun and I became a geography expert. We learned how to read road maps so well we could figure out the mileage to the next rest stop. It was a necessity. One summer we went all the way down the west coast right from Vancouver all the way down through to Tijuana, Mexico. Stopping at various places on route.

We took trips to the interior of BC, in the Okanogan. I learned about the Fraser Canyon, the many tunnels, and how the trains work through the region. About landslides, Rogers Pass, the Trans-Canada Highway, and rapids below. Travelling all the time and learning how to basically travel. We had a lot of fun learned how to swim in various hotel pools. And down at the beach learning how to swim. So the swimming was a big thing.

While I was in the boy scouts I had a job cutting grass. I used the money I earned to pay for a trip to England for a Boy Scout Royal Jamboree and some traveling around England. I checked out my family roots. Learned how everything fit in. It was a real hoot running around there. We did the continent, we did southern England, and Europe all the way Venice.

One summer I came home and told my family I'm building a sailboat. Hearing this, my dad came home with rudder parts to use for the project. Suddenly I started learning all about sailboats. Then he managed to get a small sail pram which could hold two kids or one adult. It's just basically about the size of a bathtub with a rudder on it. It was a big deal. He taught me how to sail these things around bleach bottles at the local lake. Also, as well as that he had a thirty footer, and we would take that out and sail up and down in between the ferry boats in Horseshoe Bay. I learned a lot and got an appreciation for sailing.

I developed mental health issues as a young adult. It was during my brief military experience. I was going through training and was sleep deprived. I arrived at the camp I was already extremely sleepy. I think it was after four days with no sleep that I just mentally checked-out. I stepped outside of myself and was jabbering away, not making a lot of sense. I had a drill sergeant up my tail and when he asked me a question, I can remember it didn't make sense. I remember that I was at a point where I was running on the mouth, looking around the room, picking flies off the wall, and decided that a bucket in the room was a fire hazard. This happened because for the previous 24 hours we were going through a fire seminar. I was just running it back through my head.

They also thought I was on drugs because I was taking acne medicine at the time. They thought I was on something else but I wasn't. I was just dead-ass tired and trying to keep up with the demands of their system. I was like a cat on a tin roof. I'm with a room full of people and I don't trust anybody. I figured everybody's going to cut my throat. I was looking over my shoulder every 30 seconds. I could not sleep in that state. So I hit the wall. I was out of it. They hobbled me off to the hospital. I admitted to the hospital on the base for a couple of days. Then they shot me down to Halifax where I was tested, the guy gave me all the tests and classified me as unfit for service.

They handcuffed me to a nurse in the back seat of a car and drove me all the way home and said to my mom, "he's yours." They thanked me for applying but gave me no prizes. All I got was a haircut and a couple of marching lessons. So that was the end of my military career. I felt depleted and totally destroyed. Myself worth went right out the window I was a failure. It was demeaning. I felt totally broken.

After my failed military experience I stayed in London and applied for a job as a driver for a tool and mold shop. But then I was lucky to run into what's probably the best mentor I've ever had. She was an old psych nurse and was designated as the special Ed teacher for Conestoga Collage in Kitchener. She was in her 80's when I met her and was quite a character. I showed up with my wallet in a complete mess, receipts and junk and everything falling out of it. She says to me "I've got you figured out in two minutes flat." I said "Well that's the quickest test I've ever taken." She got me to do some relaxation exercises and got me working out at the Y. With some physical activity and the relaxation I was all set.

Then I met my ex-wife. We lived in St. Thomas. I worked hard to support her. She always wanted to keep up with her family. I took out a mortgage on a three bedroom house. Bought two cars. Looked after the kids as they went to school. Then I got canned from work, and the wife got ticked-off about it. Next thing I know, I find out she's filling divorce papers. She wants money lots of money. Thousands of dollars disappeared out of our joint bank account. She is basically just tearing me apart. Suddenly a boyfriend shows up out of nowhere at the kids Christmas recital. I got a lawyer, paid the child support, jumped into a new business ventured, a glass repair operation. I tried to carry-on but then everything fell apart for me. My health, both physically and mentally and my finances. So I hit the wall a second time. That was when I started coming to Canadian Mental Health Association Middlesex (CMHA).

At CMHA I received support looking for work and getting involved with the programs that were offered. Maybe 3, 4 months. I saw it as an opportunity. I was working again independently. The sales were good enough to pay the bills. I wasn't getting rich but I made a profit. It was a cold day in the winter. There were no sales I had no money I was behind the eight-ball. Emotionally I was a wreck. Physically I was a wreck. So I turned to Ontario Works (OW). They finally relented and got me somebody who understood disabilities. She recognized right away that there was more to me than just a regular application. I was dealing with depression and so it was again suggested that I get some support from CMHA.

It took me here a year and half to basically get myself back together. What I've come to realize is the following: hospitalization feels terrible it is demeaning. I know I felt like a failure, which is false I am not a failure because of mental health issues. I thought you could not have mental illness unless you were diagnosed, I believed it was my learning disability that caused all my issues. I was trying to cope with it as best as possible and be given some coping strategies by some of the professionals I had run into. But I had not been accommodating and so soon my mental health also became a challenge.

However, there is one thing I want to highlight. While I was facing all the many issues in my life I always managed to keep up the DJ work I was doing. It meant so much to me. It lifted my emotions, to be able to go out play good music and to be the center of attention in a positive way for a little while.

The showmanship and the artistic talent that was released every time I went out and worked a gig. Basically I was playing a list of music, but I had to use and know many different types of media from: 8 track tapes, to vinyl records, to dragging around a bunch of cassette tapes, to finally CD's, and then digital. I had to adapt and roll through those changes. I needed to stay technologically ahead of the game. And I am proud to say I did. I have lots of stories which are connected to my DJ'ing. Lots of stories. I could bend your ear forever. But I will stay on track here and say that since this last bout mental illness I have been on the way up since.

Today I'm just dealing with today, and getting used to the medication I am on. At first I was literally in a dizzy state for almost a month, it was hard to preserver. It was giving me heavy headaches and I put on weight. But I've managed to drop a bit of weight so I'm feeling a lot healthier. I am involved with a lot of the physical programs that CMHA offer. So that's the positive experiences. And that's the big leap forward. I feel I am getting back on track. I just feeling good.

I now meditate and practice relaxation. It is surprising really how little bothers me now. I don't stutter, I'm on top of things, I am creative, I got the answers for things that people didn't even think of. People are going how do you know that? I might have had some learning issues and mental health issues but I also have a high IQ.

That has not changed. I feel I am on top of this thing and can manage.

I am also spending more time with my brother who's now retired. It grounds me. He did funny things like jumping out of helicopters and running around with Canada's navy. It's a magical thing this kind of stuff. I wanted to get into with getting into with doing air craft. I always had a kind of a love for it. So I wanted to mess around with planes and stuff, but I never got my chance. But his experiences kind of rub off on me and so I live it through him. I seem to have calmed down. Even in stressful situations, I can stop and think, what I am doing.

I have goals now. I want to work towards going back to work. I want to improve on my social skills. I would like to find a partner so look out girls I'm coming after you. I have to admit to myself though, there's more desire there than actual ability. I am not sure a woman would want to be involved with a man who does not have a car and so rides a bicycle to get around. On a date the best I can do right now is McDonald's. You know I do think it will work but I will have to wait and see.

So, life is not easy but if you do the right things in the right order with the right tools and the right programs, success will come. I've actually had some experiences where it was the right person, right time and everything, a lot of things were good, but I wasn't even close to ready. It seems to be my way that success is so close but then for some reason I always shoot myself in the leg, and I never the get the chance to be successful. The opportunities are dangling in front of me, the brass-ring is right there, but I just can't jump high enough.

I still have some regrets that I am working through. I still regret the fact that I don't have regular contact with my two sons. And when I do it is awkward. I am not really sure why, but I do know I am having a tough time with it.

Mental Illness and How it has Impacted my Life: The Story of Rose Mary Arnold

I was first diagnosed with a mental illness at 19 years of age, but I always knew something was wrong, especially at the age of eight.

When I was eight years old I had a cruel teacher and I would cry most of the night with thoughts of having to face her again the next day. My mom was so concerned that she took me to see a psychiatrist at The Children's Psychiatric Institute (CPRI). The psychiatrist thought it might be good for me to go into the in-patient program and to begin treatment with medication. My mom, bless her heart, flatly refused and we went home. Mom was a very strong, proud, protector of her disabled brood. My father was in a wheelchair with paraplegia, my brother was deaf, and I had both hyperactivity and depression. I am not sure, but maybe I got scared straight, as we never went back to CPRI, and my life seemed to improve for a time.

When we moved from the London community of Northridge to Byron my life seemed to turn itself around, at least for the first year; I seemed to thrive emotionally. That grade six year I was fortunate enough to have an absolute saint for a teacher, I owe him everything, and will never forget him.

My teacher looked and acted like Kramer from the Seinfeld television show, and made us laugh all day long with his wonderful stories, especially those of Europe. He was amazing and I honestly believe he saved my life with his humour. For me life went from being a crying jag the year before to a party that never seemed to end. Even the kids in my school liked me, for the most part, and I was chosen as umpire on their baseball team every recess that spring. I was having a Gabrielle Roy (author of *Enchanted Summer*) kind of summer that year, even having made a few friends.

But high school would find me sad and lonely and longing for my favourite teacher's class again. I hid in my room listening to my radio and wouldn't come out. I would lay in my bed spinning stories of how I wished my life could be, in my own little world, where I would live in my own mansion on the water, or be skiing in Banff all day. I managed to get out of bed and study a little bit, and pulled OK marks. Still I was terrifying my parents with all the time I spent alone, and how I wanted to keep the door to my room shut all the time. It was becoming a family battle. My mom was constantly threatening to take my bedroom door off. My dad, who was always wanting to make peace, would try to coax me out to go with going to the movies or out to dinner. I was like a circus act to my brother, as he would ridicule me to our relatives and friends who would come to visit. Still, I wouldn't come out of my room: I preferred to be alone and make up stories in my head.

Then, when I was eighteen, turning nineteen, my world fell apart. I lost total touch with reality and thought that everyone was out to kill me. My boyfriend, who is now my husband, was the only one besides my parents who stayed by my side. He was my only true friend. I was terrified.

With a diagnosis of schizophrenia I was hospitalized for three long months. But it wasn't all bad. I met someone who taught me a lot about writing and journaling. I was hospitalized several times over the years. My diagnosis of schizophrenia was changed to bipolar disorder by my psychiatrist.

My psychiatrist isn't much on talk, but he sure knows a lot about bipolar disorder. He knows that when I am manic, which is much of the time, I need peace and quiet. He knows that I get over stimulated in crowds or when there are too many people around. My psychiatrist also understands that when I am manic I can tend to run off at the mouth and not understand that what I have said hurts people. This is another reason I do not have a lot of friends. I can act a little weird at times and sometimes my laughter and antics set me apart.

After my Mom died in 2008, I had a very bad psychotic episode. I could see tanks going down my neighborhood streets. I also thought I could drive to my aunt's cottage on Lake Papineau. Instead, I ended up in a ditch. After the car accident I spent four months in hospital. I never thought I would end up at St. Joseph's Health Care London at the London Psychiatric Hospital (now referred to as Parkwood Mental Health Care Center). My mom had always insisted on taking me home until I got better.

I know it was the stress that broke me. I had given birth prematurely to my daughter and at the same time my mom had a very serious stroke. Mom could not talk or move. I felt helpless and so alone. Before my Mom got sick I was so excited to be pregnant. I daydreamed about Mom and Dad and the baby and me and my husband. Now my world was truly upside down. Dad also wound up in Parkwood Hospital with a broken hip. This meant I was driving from University Hospital to see my Mom to St. Joseph's Hospital to see my daughter, and then over to Parkwood Hospital to see my dad. I could hardly get out of bed I was so depressed. Then I got manic and was saying things to the nurses and health care professionals that were pretty shocking.

I had been in my psychiatrist's pregnancy study. All I could think was, I have to stay well for my daughter's sake; but in my mania, Children's Aid Society (CAS) became involved.

My mental health issues had always been an embarrassment to my family. And now I too was embarrassed. As my few friends not only questioned me as a person, they also began to wonder how able I was to be a mother. They would say I was different when I have a mental illness. Then when I turned to them for support, the CAS was called in pretty quickly. As I look back I realize I needed my mom, I needed to be mothered. But I also realize I felt the burn of stigmatization by my friends and the sting of the system. In time, my young family would be reunified and my daughter would come home.

When we were at my daughter's discharge meeting, the head doctor, who was playing with his pen at the time, said "We think it would be in the best interest of the child to go into foster care." My good friend disagreed. In fact she felt so passionately about the idea that we might lose our daughter that she decided to move in with us to help. She decided she would stay until everything was figured out. She knew that in time we would be fine and able to parent our daughter properly. I wasn't so sure: she had more confidence in me than I did in myself. She really fought for my husband and me.

At the time I felt that the CAS was out to destroy us. Our daughter was born on July 6th, but wasn't able to come home until October. She was finally able to breathe and eat without a nasogastric tube and a breathing tube. But by March, she refused to eat by bottle, and had to have a gastric tube surgically placed into her stomach. She was deemed a failure to thrive, and we were blamed. Once again the CAS took her from us.

This event was my worst experience of prejudice and discrimination. I blamed myself. I thought I have bipolar disorder, therefore I am not worthy of ever being a good mother. I questioned myself, my marriage, and everything and everyone around me. We had to get a lawyer, who cost us a lot of money, and we lost our daughter for a whole year. She was eventually returned. Since then, I have come to accept that the CAS will be in our lives. But I'm always looking over my shoulder and I let my husband do a lot of her care now. This puts my marriage on shaky ground. The two of us blame each other for what went on that year. I always feel deep down that it would have been easier to cope with cancer than be cursed with Bipolar Disorder.

As I stated earlier, I lost both my parents at a critical time in my life. However, I have learned to carry on from my many losses. I try to live each day as it comes, knowing that some days I feel heavy depression, and other days I am highly excitable with mania.

We have a few support workers that come in to care for our daughter, as her needs are complex, and the older she gets the stronger she gets. I feel the system is kinder to us now. The CAS checks in from time to time, but realizes how hard our child's care really is.

I most want to help other mothers who might be facing the decision to place their kids in Foster Care or not. I want to fight to keep them with their families like my good friend fought and won for us. How grateful I am to have a daughter of my own. Though she has many disabilities, she also has abilities. She has taught me many things.

Whenever I look back over the years, I think about sixth grade and how kind my teacher was to me, and how he taught me to live again. That year taught me to get back up and carry on.

A Moment of Clarity: The Story of Scott Johnson

I can share a story about mental illness. A few years back I was walking through the halls of Victoria Hospital. I was on my way to see my psychiatrist and I ran into someone I had attended high school with. We were talking and in time he switched the conversation. He said, "Yeah you should see all of these fruitcakes on the seventh floor." Then he asked me "What are you doing here?" I was not going to say that I was here to see my psychiatrist. Instead I remember thinking as I stood there listening to him continue with, "you can tell those mentally ill people, I see them all the time," that I was one of those people. By that point in time I had even spent many weeks on the seventh floor as I healed from my illness. I made some excuse for being there like a specialist appointment. I haven't seen this guy since high school. There was no way I was going to spill my guts to him. So I was like "Yeah ok." It made me realize that I held the same view before I admitted to hospital for a mental illness.

On five different occasions I have been hospitalized due to my mental health illness. Seems like when it rains it pours.

In 2009 I was miserable. I felt like my life was awful and would never get better. I was living with my father and my grandmother at the time. I wrote a note, took all my father's sleeping medication and went to bed. In hindsight I know I was lucky that my dad found me when he did. I have been told that if I had been left for another 15 or 20 minutes I would have died. But back then, when I woke up in the hospital I was a far cry from being grateful.

Waking up in the hospital I remember I was so angry. It was my plan to die and that is what I intended to do. They had to put me in restraints due to my anger. As well I didn't hit it off with the doctor who was assigned to my case. I didn't like him. So I didn't talk to him at all. About anything. I just denied that I had wanted to die and told everyone I was fine now. I guess it worked since I was discharged after only five days. I know now I just wasn't ready to admit anything was wrong with me.

After my first hospitalization I returned home. I lived with my dad and grandmother. I remember when I got home my dad, grandmother, and I all acted as if nothing had happened. I just went back into my room and simply resumed my regular routine. My grandmother had made it clear that there was nothing really wrong with me. My dad said nothing. We all just forgot about it.

A few months later a grand mal seizure put me back into the hospital. I had a MRI which uncovered a spot on my brain. I was all upset about that, really scared. They did the test a second time but the doctors could not identify what it was. I was sent home with no answers for the seizure. I ended up deeply depressed again. I didn't want to be around anymore.

At home I went out to the balcony of our apartment. We lived on the 12th floor. I planned on jumping. The police came, the negotiators were there and I don't know if I lost my nerve or what but then I noticed there were people; residents from the building all around watching me. They even brought their kids. Everyone was looking up at me.

I had intended to jump and end my life but there were children down there. I was standing on the ledge and there was a policemen talking to me and I'm looking out and I'm like "What the fuck is wrong with you people? They are little kids. They can't see this." All these thoughts were going through my head. If I jumped these kids are going to see me and they're going to remember it forever. So that's what triggered me to get down and go with the policeman. All I could think of was "What the hell kind of parent brings their kid out to see someone jump from the 12th floor?" I guess I had a moment of clarity there and realized that I did not want to do that to those little kids. They would never forget it.

The police were kind to me but I was back in the hospital with that same doctor I had previously. I refused to talk to him for three days that time. I don't know why I didn't like him. I can't explain it. I just thought he was a jerk. I didn't like him at all.

After I was released from the hospital everything went well for a while. Then I had a brief episode again. I needed someone to talk to so I turned to my grandmother. I know the smarter thing would have been to phone the crisis line and speak to one of the workers. But for some unknown reason I turned to my grandmother. I was pretty upset about something and I guess with my past suicide attempt she got overwhelmed and over reacted thinking I was again suicidal. But I really wasn't. She called the police and they took me back to the hospital. I was interviewed by the police officers. I guess I had said something about previously being on the ledge of the balcony and he took that to mean that was what I was going to do this time as well. I ended up on a form. This time I had a different psychiatrist and she was really nice. She's like "You're not suicidal, you're just having a bad day." She sent me home.

It is funny how everything goes alright for a while and then it all goes to hell. A perfect storm brewed for me back in May of 2011. At that time we had to put our dog to sleep which was very hard on me. At the same time my father was diagnosed with brain cancer. And my grandmother was diagnosed with stomach cancer. So within a span of about three weeks I found out that my dog, my father, and grandmother were going to pass away. I knew when they passed I would also lose my home. I had never lived on my own, so that was a very tough time.

Within a span of a couple weeks, I went from doing OK to all of a sudden everything's gone.

I had to find an apartment. I was on Ontario Works at the time so had a limited income. Both my father and grandmother were in hospital and I was alone in the apartment we all shared, and it started to sink in. One loss after another. Again I started to feel hopeless. Thinking that my life would never get any better. I have poor impulse control. So I went to the liquor store and I got a couple of bottles and came home. I took all of the medication I could find in the house and drank both bottles of liquor. Before the drugs and alcohol took over I wrote my suicide note. I went into the living room where we had an anchor in the ceiling to hang plants from. I got an extension cord and I made a noose. I was drunk obviously, and the drugs were starting to kick in. I tied a noose and then I secured it up on the ceiling. I stepped on a chair and stepped off. I have no other memory until the next day.

I am told that my sister and aunt came over to check in on me and they found. I guess that the extension cord had broken and I had fallen and I cracked my head open on the entertainment center. So they found me laying on the floor in the living room. I ended up back in the hospital and I was there for about seven weeks.

Homeless and in the hospital. My sister was so upset with me that she did not come and visit me while I was in the hospital. That was stressful. I thought maybe she would not want anything to do with me again. And that she would not allow me to see my nieces and nephews. My sister wouldn't talk to me for about a month after I was released from the hospital. I was lucky she did not disown me. In time we were able to repair our relationship. We are still fairly close. Still I know it has put a lot of worry and stress on her. I know she worries about me.

My grandmother on the other hand would have nothing more to do with me. Her final days in the hospital she wouldn't let me see her. She passed away without me ever getting to see her. My father, he was in another hospital from my grandmother and me. By the time I was recovered enough to go and visit him the cancer was so bad that he could no longer talk.

I was in hospital for about seven weeks. The psychiatrist slowly helped me to figure things out. It was a big transition from living with my dad and grandmother to live on my own. The CMHA housing advocate who worked at the hospital helped me find an apartment. Both my doctor and the advocate helped me fill out the forms I needed to so that I could receive Ontario Disability Support (ODSP.) I found a place in Central London. Nothing too fancy. It was just a little room. It had a little kitchenette with a small stove, and a bar-refrigerator. I had to share the bathroom with the other people who lived there. It was a pretty gross place. But at the time it was my first apartment so for me it was alright.

After I was discharged I started with the day program that was held at the hospital. Every day I went from nine until three in the afternoon. Everyone who attended had been recently discharged from the hospital due to a mental illness. In the day program we worked on life skills and crisis management. I found that very helpful and after that I would go visit my father in the hospital. My father passed away in September of 2011.

Over the years I have noticed there seems to be a stigma towards mental illness; and it seems to me to be a pretty prevalent thing. My family and I believed that view. You know if you have a mental illness then you must be a nut case. And so at first the person with a mental illness will struggle because they do not want to be the crazy one. I struggle with that myself. Thinking there's nothing really wrong with me. It's just all in my head. Then realizing it has happened to me in my own journey. It is just fear fueled by stigma.

Mental health issues are not really a disease like cancer. Mental illness is not prejudice, it can happen to anyone. It has nothing to do with your age, your income level, or your level of education. Anyone can suffer with it. Your neighbor or even the person next to you on the bus. I have meant people that I would not in a million years think they struggled with mental health issues and have been hospitalized like myself.

Compared to where I was back in 2009 when this whole journey began I know I am much, much, better. There is still a lot of guilt for me for all the things I have done. I guess I just have to remember it was not my fault and try to understand that it is a brain chemistry thing. My wife has been a big support for me. Likewise I no longer deny it. I have also realized I need to talk to someone. I have a really good psychiatrist now who I can talk too. I believe this is one of the main reasons I am recovered. He is great and I feel I have been very fortunate with the team that now surrounds me. It is helpful for me to understand myself and why I do the things I do. I realized I needed to stop lying to myself and face the truth about these things.

Nickel for a Noun: Author Es (Scott Billias)

The last few days have been the weirdest days ever

Funny, how rough times can change for the better.

Started out on my bike, bringing back those empty bottles

Some Nissan in my blind spot turns left at full throttle.

Their crew must have been late for a dinner reservation

'Cause this maroon cut me off with no clue or hesitation.

Guess my survival's not as important as a seat at their table,

Does it count I'm an adult outcast who's disabled?

Screech to a halt to avoid a near-miss

Chick in the backseat notices and tries to diss.

Check my body for injuries, glass has lost returnability

So my grand total dropped to one-thirty from one-seventy.

Make it to Labatt's with like a minute before they close

Grab my loose change and notice pain from my thumb to my elbow.

So I use my bottle score to dial 911.

Ask for an ambulance, but next move was a dumb one.

Filed a traffic report, not even finished triage

Seeing about an x-ray to analyze this damage.

Witness report completed with my full name and address

Yet that's what gives the punk pig an entry point of access.

He runs the names I was given through his computer system.

A pop-up for priors and an outstanding warrant

You could have contacted my lawyer if it was really that important.

So after a night of rancid water and bars of nutri-grain

In courthouse holdings singing "Hallowed be thy Name."

The drunk in the next cell doesn't like my rendition

What's wrong with Iron Maiden? It's a song about prison!

Now I'm at a loss again, in county jail processing

Huge dude with braids is telling me to take my clothes off.

Shower thoroughly 'cause your smell pisses me off, Scott.

Balls just got wet, I get the best reality check

From an African C.O. I literally just met.

He said, "this ain't you...choose how you will do...stay true... Respect
when its due."

That's what I construed.

I'm almost at the brink, because I'm in the clink.

Suicide watch since they won't let me see my shrink.

Multiple crown hearings, sanity disappearing.

Forest of negativity, no meds to carve a clearing.

Hearing Metallica through a ghetto-blaster.

My obedience does not make you my master!

Skipped my dinner tray. Much to my dismay.

Threw away the form so the chaplain would visit me.

Guards don't know that my sentence is getting diverted.

Need some priestly advice, don't want to be converted.

Like how you make amends to a no-contact order?

How you visit family across another border?

Learned a great deal through it all, such as who answers their collect calls.

Whatever You Think
You Will Be: The Story
of Tom Mood

Physically I have always been in good shape. Back when my mental health issues began to bother me I was running a couple times a day and swimming three or four times a day. Maybe that is why I did not get treated for a mental illness sooner, because I was so active. But really all that energy was me being weighed down by my illness.

My employment history began when I was 12 years of age. I was a Telegram-Paperboy. That was when I started to notice that something was wrong with me because I could not keep all the papers organized. My real dream job was to work in the greenhouse in my community. I had a love of nature. I still do. Nature calms me and I see its beauty. At the time, I also meant a man in his 70's who would talk to me about poetry and would give me advice about writing. To this day I still remember a lot of his advice.

Today I am a poet/writer and often nature will be the topic of my poetry. I thought working in the green houses would be a wonderful way to earn a living. But I guess they could tell that I was not a good fit since I struggled to keep up. They would not hire me. But I wanted a job and that is how I landed at the chemical plant in Tillsonburge. They offered me a job and I accepted. I wanted to earn a living. It was import to both me and my family that I did. When I look back to the time I worked in the plant, I realize that it was not a good job for me. It moved too fast. That place ruined me in so many ways.

My mental illness really amplified while I was working at the chemical plant. It felt like I had something in my head that seemed to be going around and around. Like a vibration that went around and around. But it really wasn't. As well as this weird vibration, I was hearing voices. Just a bit, so it seemed like they were off in the distance. It felt like I was also losing supports in my head for my eyes. Not like they would fall out of my head just like they were no longer supported. It felt peculiar and scary. Today I believe that was due to the toxins from the chemical plant where I worked. I think they ruined my eyes. I could still see but there was just a strange feeling. And in time I lost my ability to concentrate. Working there harmed me in so many ways, I know that now.

A bit later, I was living at the YMCA. I lived there for about two years. I was not getting along with some of the other guys who lived there. I had touched someone gently and the guy wanted me to be charged with assault. But I was not doing anything wrong. While I lived at the Y I tried working at the Holiday Inn but I was not fast enough. I washed dishes. While I worked that dishwashing job I accidentally cut my hand. I refused to look after the wound. It got badly infected and so I needed to take time off work for it to heal. I had to receive Workman's Compensation. Now I think I was using the wound as a cry for help really. My mental health issues were becoming more troublesome. I was not really feeling very good at the time.

I was having a hard time because of the voices in my head. While living at the YMCA I attempted suicide by stabbing myself. I used a small knife. My best friend, who also lived there found me and he applied pressure to the wound. I was taken to the hospital emergency and rather than keep me the hospital sent me home. I could not get the help I needed.

I moved back in with my parents and our relationship became challenged. All of us were doing the best we could but we did not really understand what was happening to me. I began to hallucinate that there was a fire in my head, and I do not know how, but people were telling me there was a fire in my head. It was getting hotter and hotter, but it wasn't real, it was just a hallucination. That was the day after I attempted suicide. I told everyone I was dead but really I was in my head. I was taken back to the hospital and this time and I was admitted. I was there for three weeks. But after my hospitalization my parents and I had a better relationship.

In 1985 I went off the medication which had been prescribed for me and had allowed me some stability. I was again hospitalized for about four weeks. From the hospital I went to live in a group home in Old South, London. I got along good with the guys there; they all liked me. I lived there for three or four weeks. After that, I got my own apartment.

My new apartment was in the Old East Village. I was there for one year. I enjoyed living there. I was paying a reasonable rent. I remember there was a hole in the roof, but it was not a problem since my dad knew a guy who could fix it for me. Then I moved into another apartment in Central London and lived there for about six years. Then I moved again to my current location and have lived there for 24 years.

My final hospitalization happened in 1995 for about four weeks. Many years before I was involved in a car accident. A van got too close to me and the mirror hit my elbow and swung me into the ditch. For years after that my spine was acting up. I was in constant sever pain and it was all twitchy. I was walking around with my back parallel to the ground. It was really painful and I was drug resistant. My doctor at the time did not believe it was the car accident. I know he is entitled to his own opinion. But I still believe it was the result of the accident. Thankfully in time I would see a new psychiatrist who would help me in my recovery.

My new doctor was an astute psychiatrist who was also a pain specialist. I began to receive the right medications that worked well for me. My pain settled and so did my mental health issues. I recovered from both. What also helped me to recover was to get busy. In other words I got a life. Today I have recovered and healed from my mental illness. I think positively. I have better concentration and am able to read again. I write well and concentrate well. I am on medications and they seem to work well.

I love to travel. Once a year since 1990 I have travelled to New Zealand to visit a friend who lives there. We meant each other in 1977 when I was 21 years old at a nature camp. I usually stay for about three weeks. We do some sightseeing and in the past I had the opportunity while there to do some trapping.

Now I have worked the same job for 22 years. I deliver flyers in my community for our local newspaper. I am also writing. I know a quote which goes like this, "Whatever you think; you will be." I have three books published; the first book I dedicated to Henry David Thoreau and Ralph Waldo Emerson, the second book I dedicated to my great uncle and Grey Owl and the third book I dedicated to my New Zealand friend. As well I have had a few of my poems published in Indigenous newspapers.

My mental illness has given my family more understanding. I have a sister who is two years older than me and a brother who is seven and a half years younger than me. Today my brother is really good with electronics. In my family I was viewed as the naturalist boy and my brother was viewed as the electronics boy. Over the last few years he has helped me often with electronics. When I was young I would keep crayfish, frogs, and turtles in pails. To this day I enjoy being outside and am amazed by nature's beauty.

My advice for anyone who is dealing with mental health issues always accept advice from your supports and be a good listener. Persevere and have faith and confidence in yourself.

Conclusion

"I teach one thing and one only: that is, suffering and the end of suffering."

The Buddha

I hope as you read through this book you were able to see the suffering and that you saw it in all its different forms. Maybe you saw individuals were on their journey of just beginning suffering, others who were right in the middle of it and hopeful those who had found a way out of their suffering.

This book contains highs and lows. Maybe at times you are laughing and other times you are reaching for the tissue box. Whatever you experienced I hope that you also realized that mental illness has a human face. It could be a family member, your neighbour, your colleague, or anybody else in your life. Mental illness strikes everyone. No one is spared. My desire is that you realized that recovery is possible as you read through the many stories in this book. But most of all I hope you realized that we have a voice and we are not afraid to use it.

By Aimee Fischer

Acknowledgements

I have to say, I am not—even at the best of times—good with conclusions. The conclusion of this book project has challenged me in every way. Still, conclusions are a natural part of life and so rather than willfully grasping on I let go and allow you, the reader the opportunity to engage with this thought-provoking book.

This Does Not Define Me: Lived Experiences of Mental Illness book project began in March of 2014. It started with a group of six individuals with a lived experience of mental health issues: John H., Warren C., Allen B., Aimee F., Jeff K., and Kristeen E.. For the next six months they worked tirelessly to define the parameters of the project and to train in conducting interviews. They began interviewing the featured individuals within the book during September 2014. Through-out the next six months 25 interviews were conducted. Jeff as our sound man was there for all 25 interviews, while John, Warren, Allen, Aimee, and Kristeen conducted the interviews. To this group of individuals I thank-you for all your hard work and creative energy. The challenge you faced was to take a vague idea and give it substance. Together the group defined the project's parameters and envisioned what the final product might look like. To all of you I want to say how much I appreciate your level of commitment to the project for without it, well it never would have come to light.

March 2015 saw the start of what I came to call stage two of the book project. Taking the recorded interviews and transcribing them verbatim. I was not sure how this would come to light. I turned to then CMHA's Director of Technology Trent Ellis for his advice. The special computer hardware he suggested would need to be purchased. At the time CMHA was facing many cut backs so I was uncertain if my Program Manager would or even could approve it. I was relieved when I got word from then Community Wellness Program Manager Kevin Dickins, that he could approve the cost. Let it be known, this project would have collapsed had Kevin denied the necessary funding needed to purchase it. With the necessary computer hardware it still took many hours of meticulous and exacting work to complete each transcript. I would like to thank both Nicole Maguire and Jessica Vanwyngarden for their dedication and expert typing.

Once a few of the transcripts were completed stage three of the book project could begin. This was when each transcript would be broken down and transformed into the story told. Those who expressed an interest in doing this part were first trained and were given an example of how to actually accomplish the transformation. There were four individuals who trained but only two decided to work the project, April R. and CN. For the next ten months both CN and April worked every Friday afternoon on the project in the CMHA computer lab. Both took care to respect the voice of each of the individuals who would be featured. I did not offer much help during those months, but I did provide the coffee, donuts, and Jazz. I know sometimes the weight of the project was great and so some singing was called for to lighten the load. We all joined in and sang along with such tunes as Nancy Sinatra's These Boots were made for Walkin, the Monkey's Daydream Believer, and Petula Clark's Downtown. Often a dance would break out and then came the laughter. Once our blood was circulating, we all got back to what we were there for. As I write this, I can almost hear and see the experience. I want both April and Colin to know I will never forget what you did for this project. The blood, sweat, and tears you both offered up.

Next came the pictures. Wednesday August 17, 2016 saw much activity and excitement as clients came together one at a time to pose for a headshot. The then Marketing Manager, Kristy Carins set aside the whole day to take the photos of each individual for their story. The day was beautiful and sunny and so we headed out side. I send much gratitude to Kristy. Her vision, as you can see, was spot on.

The following stage of the project began June 2017. A professional editor took on the task of taking each of the prepared manuscripts and perfecting them. This was another painstaking task which took many hours. Thank-you CM for finding a way to respect the voice of each individual featured while still creating a clean manuscript.

And then the time came to put together a cover for the book. I would like to thank Edward Platero of Platero Visual who agreed to shoot the cover. He took care to get a feeling for the project and to ask the clients: who were to pose for the shot, their ideas. It was a wonderful morning, offering an experience which will be remembered. I would also like to thank Cassandra Harris, who was our digital designer and worked the cover art.

The final stage of the book project was the planning of the Book Launch Celebration. A subcommittee of clients spent the many months prior to the January 31, 2018 event getting the particulars figured out. A huge thank-you to Aimee Fischer, CN, and Robert Chatterson for their commitment and hard work. As well as the clients help came help from the Community Wellness Programs. From the Directors Susan Macphail and Elsa Lammers, the Program Managers (there were three during the project; Kevin Dickins, Kristy Bell, and Brent Carr) the Administrative Supports Jenna Coutemanche and Denise Duncan to my team mates, Crystal McKeller, Michelle Philips, Afsaneh Aziz, Jessica Carswell, Carolyn Petley, and Trix VanEgmond. You all surrounded me when I felt overwhelmed and reminded me that everything would be alright.

I would also like to acknowledge the love and support I received from my daughter Hannah Baker, my son Angus Baker, and my sister Shelley Ballantyne. There were many car rides or cups of coffee where they listened mindfully and supportively as I unloaded my worries, my excitement, or my impatience with the project. I cannot forget my mom Dorothy or my dad Gerry Ballantyne. They are my cheerleading team who throughout the project and my life have encouraged me to follow my passions.

Finally, I will conclude with the most obvious of acknowledgements by thanking everyone who agreed to share their lived experience of mental illness. You are all strong and brave individuals. I think of you as spiritual warriors, fighting stigma and prejudice that can no longer be tolerated. Over the last three years I suspect there were times when you might have wondered if the project was going to see completion. Your patience has been appreciated as all the different pieces were worked through.

Respectfully,

Holly Ballantyne- Mental Health Worker: Community Wellness Programs, CMHA Middlesex

Made in the USA
Columbia, SC
16 February 2018